THE ROAD TO HOLLYWOOD

THE ROAD TO HOLLYWOOD

My 40-year Love Affair with the Movies

by BOB HOPE
and Bob Thomas

Doubleday & Company, Inc., Garden City, New York   1977

The authors are grateful to the following for the photographs:
MCA-Universal, Warner Bros., MGM,
United Artists, Cinerama Releasing Co.

Library of Congress Cataloging in Publication Data. Hope, Bob, 1903–   The road to Hollywood. 1. Hope, Bob, 1903– . 2. Comedians—United States—Biography. I. Thomas, Bob, 1922–   joint author. II. Title. PN2287.H63A325 791'.092'4 [B]. ISBN: 0-385-02292-1. Library of Congress Catalog Card Number 73–81988.

Book design by Beverley Gallegos

CONTENTS

WHERE THERE'S LIFE
by Bob Hope

I didn't get to Hollywood as early as B.C.*

When he first arrived, there was hardly anyone in Hollywood but a bunch of Indians waiting for John Wayne to show up.

Cecil B. De Mille was a prop boy.

George Jessel was going steady with Ramona.

Of course I would have come to Hollywood sooner, except that I had an accident.

It was called a screen test.

But now I'm getting ahead of my story, I'd better begin at the beginning.

This book is subtitled "My 40-Year Love Affair with the Movies." That's the first mistake.

The truth is that I've been in love with the movies much longer than the forty years plus I've been appearing in them.

The romance started in Cleveland when I was a small boy. Whenever I could scrape together a dime by doing odd jobs (not *that* odd!), I'd hurry down to the Alhambra or the Park movie house. I sat in the dark for hours, watching the flickering shadows on the screen. I could see myself as Rudolph Valentino, racing over the sands on horseback with Agnes Ayres in my arms. Or

* Bing Crosby, crooner, father, and member of the Lewis and Clark expedition.

Wally Reid behind the wheel of a mile-long Duesenberg. Or Richard Barthelmess winning World War I singlehandedly.

But my special favorite was Charlie Chaplin.

I sat in the darkened theater and laughed until my sides ached. It amazed me how one little guy with a funny mustache, derby, baggy suit, and cane could evoke so much laughter.

If he could do it, I could do it!

I borrowed an old suit from an older brother, a pair of brogans and a derby from my father, smudged some stove blacking on my upper lip, fashioned a cane from a tree limb, and waddled down the street to the firehouse at the end of our block. I was the hit of Euclid Street.

It wasn't long before I was discovered—by my brothers.

The Hope boys had become known for their ability to make a fast buck, and they saw me as their meal ticket. Before I could say "I don't wanna go in show business," they had me entered in a Charlie Chaplin imitation contest at Luna Park. When the judge's hand was held over my head, the applause was thundering. It helps to have six brothers.

It didn't take me long to realize that show business was for me. Especially when my schoolteachers kept telling me there was no other hope.

Many years later, I was talking to Walt Disney about his boyhood in Kansas City and mine in Cleveland. I was amazed to learn that he also got his start in show business by doing imitations of Charlie Chaplin. Walt told me he won $2 in prize money at the Rialto Theater in Kansas City. After that he teamed with a friend named Walter Pfeiffer in a comedy act for amateur nights at the local theaters and schools.

Having had his fill of the footlights, Walt went straight. I didn't.

It was another silent-screen comic who helped me land my first real break in show business.

I had worked up a dance act with a neighborhood pal, Lloyd Durbin. We could fool the public enough to land a booking at the Bandbox Theater in Cleveland. Roscoe (Fatty) Arbuckle was on the same bill.

He had been another of my idols when I was young. He had a comically expressive face and amazing agility, considering his bulk. When he did a pratfall, it was like a sequoia taking a tumble.

Arbuckle had fallen on bad times. He had been accused of manslaughter in the death of a party girl in San Francisco. Even though he had been acquitted, the public uproar made him unemployable in Hollywood. He had been one of the movies' biggest stars, and now he was touring vaudeville houses to make a buck.

I had never met a movie star before, and I was thrilled to be on the same bill with Arbuckle. Between shows, he called Lloyd and me to his dressing room.

"You boys are pretty good," he said.

"We are?" I replied in amazement.

"I think so," said Arbuckle. "The audience thinks so, too. I've got a friend here in Cleveland named Fred Hurley. He produces tab shows. If you'd like, I'll ask him if he can find a spot for you boys in one of his shows."

"Gee, Mr. Arbuckle, would you?" I said.

"Sure thing, kid," he replied. "You're ready for it."

He was true to his word. He recommended us to Fred Hurley, producer of the tabs, which were small revues that toured the vaudeville circuits. Lloyd and I were hired for a show called "Hurley's Jolly Follies." First we played the Spiegelberg Time and then we graduated to the Gus Sun Circuit. Now I was in the big time, making $40 a week.

Those years in vaudeville were the best education an entertainer could have. If you could make it on the Gus Sun Circuit, it was the equivalent of summa cum laude from Harvard. I did everything—sing, tap dance, eccentric dance, play straight man, Irish comic, Italian dialect, comedy sketches. I even played the saxophone.

Remember the old joke about the man who breaks his hand and asks the doctor, "Can I play the piano after the hand heals?" The doctor says yes, and the man says, "That's great—I never could play the piano before!"

That was me and the saxophone. I still can't play it, but I almost convinced those audiences on the Gus Sun Circuit that I was another Jimmy Dorsey. Almost.

About ten years after I met Fatty Arbuckle—he had died in 1933, probably of a broken heart—I had an encounter with another great movie comedian.

Harry Langdon had been another favorite of mine. He had been the gentlest of the comics, a baby-faced bumbler who drew enormous sympathy when things happened to him, which was often.

I found myself playing on the same vaudeville bill with Langdon at Proctor's Theater in Newark. Again it was a sad encounter with a boyhood idol.

Like Arbuckle, Langdon had lost his movie career and taken to the vaudeville circuits to earn a living. In Langdon's case, I learned later, he had done himself in by masterminding his own pictures. He had forgotten that a clever little guy named Frank Capra had directed the best Langdon features.

One day between shows, Langdon told me: "Young man, if you ever go out to Hollywood and become a star—and I think you could—don't make my mistake. Don't try to convince yourself that you're a genius."

The thought has never occurred to me. Well, hardly ever.

After I came into pictures, I realized what a collaborative effort film making is. I always tried to place myself in the hands of the best creative minds, the best technicians. I never made Harry Langdon's mistake in believing that movies are a do-it-yourself project.

My first movie test was a big hit.

Sort of a combination of the Johnstown Flood and Hurricane Agnes.

It happened in 1930, when I was playing the Orpheum Time with my partner, Louise Troxell. We had been touring the West Coast and we landed in Los Angeles to play the Hillstreet Theater. I received a telephone call from a man I'd never known before. He said his name was William Perlberg, and he was a Hollywood agent. Later he became a successful producer.

"I haven't caught your act yet, but Al Boasberg says you're great," Bill remarked.

"He did, huh? That's just because I'm using his material." Al was a top vaudeville comedy writer, and he had helped me with my act.

"How'd you like to make a screen test? The studios have been buying a lot of new talent since the talkies came in."

"A screen test? Let's see, I have a little time between my closing at the Hillstreet and my opening in San Diego. I think I could work it in."

Bill wasn't deceived by my nonchalance. He told me to report to Pathé Studios the day after I closed at the Hillstreet.

Louise and I took a taxi out to Culver City, and I performed my vaudeville act before the cameras. The crew seemed terribly amused, and I flew off to the date in San Diego—this was before airlines were flying there. I was certain that I was going to be Cleveland's gift to the motion picture world.

My confidence began to crack when I didn't hear from Bill Perlberg about the test. When Louise and I finished the appearance in San Diego and returned to Los Angeles, I called him.

"What about the test?" I asked.

I could tell by the silence at the other end of the line that it hadn't exactly turned out like *Ben-Hur*.

"Do you really want to see it?" Perlberg asked.

"Certainly!"

I still had a shred of confidence when I strolled on the Pathé lot to see the test in a projection room. The projectionist had all the enthusiasm of Ned Sparks. "Do you want to look at it?" he asked.

"Sure I do! That's what I'm here for."

"Okay," he shrugged.

I sat in the darkened projection room all alone. When I made my first entrance, my nose came on the screen ten minutes before the rest of my face. I couldn't believe how bad I was. I felt as if I were watching some other comic I didn't know. And didn't want to.

When the lights came on in the projection room, I wished I could vanish into the woodwork. It had been a new and shattering experience—to see myself as others see me. I had never seen myself in vaudeville, and I could convince myself that I was boffola. But there I was, in glorious black and white up there on the movie screen, and I was awful!

I slunk out of the projection room and sneaked down the studio streets like a SMERSH agent in a James Bond movie. Too embarrassed to walk out the studio gate, I tried to climb over the wall. I failed at that, too.

It was fully a week before I regained my confidence.

After my flop in Culver City, I hustled back East determined to make a bum of Horace Greeley.

New York was good to me. I finally got to play the Palace. To a vaudevillian, that was the equivalent of the World Series, the Super Bowl, and moving into the White House as a steady resident.

The Palace led to my first Broadway musical, *Ballyhoo of 1932*, and then came *Roberta*.

It was a beautiful show, with a score of hits by Jerome Kern and Otto Harbach, and a cast that included George Murphy, Fay Templeton, Tamara, Ray Middleton, Sydney Greenstreet, and a sax player named Fred MacMurray.

Both George and Fred were tabbed for the movies, and so was I. Paramount wanted me to appear in *Sitting Pretty* with Ginger Rogers and Jack Oakie. I was told about the deal by my agent, Louie Shurr, also known as the Doctor.

"Bob, the producer is Charlie Rogers, and he's willing to go two thousand a week on a four-week guarantee," Doc said. "It looks like a good opportunity—might lead to a term contract with Paramount."

"Hollywood—who needs it?" I replied. "I'm doing okay in New York."

That wasn't sheer bravado on my part. *Roberta* was a smash, and I was being sought for other Broadway shows. Between productions, I could play vaudeville in the movie houses. I was beginning to appear as guest star on radio shows. And I had an offer to make some comedy shorts in New York.

So I was able to thumb my nose at Hollywood. With my nose, that's a lot of thumbing!

The offer for the movie shorts came from Educational, which made two-reelers at a studio in Astoria, Long Island. The producer, Jack Skirball, was willing to give me $2,500 per short, and I was supposed to make six of them. I could work in *Roberta* at night and make the shorts in the daytime.

"I'll take it," I told the good Doctor—he was called that because of his ability to minister to ailing Broadway shows.

The first comedy was called *Going Spanish*. Leah Ray appeared opposite me, and the director was Al Christie, who had started making movies in 1909. The plot was not exactly *Mourning Becomes Electra*. My big scene came when I swallowed some Mexican jumping beans and leaped around the scenery like a drunken kangaroo.

The short was booked to play at the Rialto Theater in New York, and I went to see it opening day. I had the same wave of nausea that I had felt in the projection room at Pathé. I wanted to run, not walk, to the nearest fire exit.

I was in a sour mood when I walked out of the Rialto and ran into Walter Winchell. I had known Walter when he was hustling ads for the *Vaudeville News*. Now he was the most-read columnist in New York.

14

Going Spanish
(with Leah Ray)

Watch the Birdie

"What are you doing here, Bob?" he asked.

"I've just been seeing my first comedy short," I confessed.

"Yeah? How was it?"

"I'll tell you how it was. When they catch John Dillinger, they're going to make him sit through it twice."

Winchell laughed and strolled down Broadway. Little did I know that he was going to print my crack verbatim. Doc Shurr received a furious phone call from Jack Skirball, production head of Educational.

"What the hell is your client doing to us?" Skirball demanded. "Bob Hope is hard enough to sell, without him running down his own picture in Winchell's column. We're through with him! We're dropping his option!"

Doc relayed the bad news to me, and he asked if I could save the contract by asking Winchell to print a retraction.

I called Walter and told him: "Your item cost me two thousand, five hundred bucks! Can't you square me with Educational?"

"How can I?" he replied. "You said it. Besides, I thought it was funny."

I was fired by Educational and hired by Warner Brothers. A producer named Sam Sax was making some comedy and musical shorts for Warner Brothers, and he hired me to star in six of them. Sam's ability to squeeze a buck could make Jack Benny seem like Aristotle Onassis. He made those shorts in three days, rain or shine. In fact, if a director got three sprocket holes behind schedule, Sam would stick his head into the sound stage and say, *"What's wrong?"*

After bombing out with Educational, I wanted to make good, and I did my best to co-operate with Sam's thrifty ways. But on one occasion I couldn't help myself.

My second short at Warners was a Pulitzer Prize drama called *The Old Grey Mayor*. It featured Lionel Stander, the actor with a voice that sounds like a sanding machine with a cold. I had a scene in which I came out of a telephone booth and ran into him. Like most of Sam Sax's scenes, I did it without rehearsal. But when I looked at Stander, I broke out in a laughing fit.

"Cut!" bawled the director. "Mr. Hope, may I remind you that the audience is supposed to laugh, not the actors. Now let's try it again."

I returned to the telephone booth and emerged to stare at Stander—and broke out laughing.

"Cut!" said the director. "Mr. Hope, have you been nipping in your dressing room? Now, *please*, let's get it right this time."

Again, failure. Soon Sam Sax came bursting through the stage door to demand what was going on.

"I can't help it," I said. "Have you ever looked at Lionel? He's got one brown eye and one blue eye! Funniest thing I've ever seen."

"Mr. Hope," said Sam, "what I'll do to you if you waste any more time will be a tragedy. There are plenty of other comedians who can read your lines."

That sobered me up in a hurry.

Much happened to me in the three years following *Roberta*. I appeared in three Broadway shows: *Say When,* with Harry Richman; *Ziegfeld Follies,* with Fanny Brice, Josephine Baker, and Gertrude Niesen; and *Red, Hot and Blue!* with Ethel Merman and Jimmy Durante. I started appearing on radio regularly, first on the Bromo Seltzer show with Al Goodman's orchestra, Jane

Froman, and James Melton, later with Shep Fields and his Rippling Rhythm Revue for Woodbury Soap. If I had any time off, I could always play vaudeville houses on the Loew's circuit.

Of course, the most important thing that happened to me during that time was my marriage to a beautiful, charming, talented, intelligent lady (okay, Dolores, you can stop reading over my shoulder).

I must in all honesty report that before Dolores happened into my life, I had become quite skilled at playing the dating game. Ah, those were the days! There I was with my name in lights, appearing in shows that featured perhaps twenty-five delightful, delovely young show girls. I had a Pierce-Arrow town car with a chauffeur, and those crazy girls kept jumping on the running board. I had to throw confetti in their faces to get rid of them.

Dolores wasn't that way at all. She was a little vague about how I was earning my living, and that's one of the things that intrigued me about her. Was she clever—or ignorant? One of these days I'm going to ask her.

Because my New York career was moving along nicely, I turned a deaf ear to movie offers. The Broadway shows, radio, vaudeville, and the movie shorts were bringing $5,000 a week, and the studios couldn't match that. Besides, Dolores wasn't enthused about my going into pictures. She thought it would break up our act.

We had a lot of fun playing the vaudeville houses. I did some of my inimitable routines, then I introduced Dolores. She had a marvelous, warm singing voice—still has—and I sat right down on the stage in front of her and listened. While she sang "Blue Moon" or "Did You Ever See a Dream Walking?" I mooned over her, touched her arm, tasted her shoulder, did everything I could to break her up. I got the laughs, she got the sympathy. (She's been getting it ever since.)

I agreed to make a test for Fox, and I must admit that the studio bosses didn't come beating at my door to sign me to a contract. That reinforced my determination to give films the go-by. RKO saw the Fox test and offered me a role with Jack Haley in *Radio City Revels.*

"Thanks but no thanks," I replied like a Grand Duke declining the caviar.

Hollywood was for peasants, I decided. New York was my town. The New Yorkers were sophisticated enough to understand and enjoy my suave, sterling style. Hollywood was hicksville.

Big Broadcast of 1938
(with Shirley Ross)

Soon I decided to join the peasants.

For my debut in feature films I can thank several people:

Vernon Duke and Ira Gershwin, who wrote "I Can't Get Started with You," which I sang to a show girl named Eve Arden in *Ziegfeld Follies* . . .

Mitchell Leisen and Harlan Thompson, the director and producer of *The Big Broadcast of 1938*, who saw me perform the song and figured I could make it in films . . .

William LeBaron, the production boss at Paramount, who agreed to take a chance on me . . .

Jack Benny, who turned down the role I ended up doing . . .

Thanks to that parlay, I was signed to a Paramount contract for three pictures a year starting at $20,000 per picture. It was a seven-year contract with options. Naturally the studio exercised

19

the options. That meant that any time during the seven years the studio could deposit you on Melrose Avenue with the rest of the trash.

With some misgivings, I headed west again. In those days, it was the custom of stars to get off the Santa Fe Chief at Pasadena instead of going on to the Los Angeles station—to avoid the mobs, you know. The studios met the stars at Pasadena in grand style.

When I stepped off the train at Pasadena, there was no block-long limousine waiting to whisk Dolores and me to a mansion in Bel Air. No dancing starlets with baskets of grapefruit. Not even a redcap with a wilted gladiola.

I made my "I'll show 'em" speech.

"I'll show 'em," I said. "I've got some money in the bank. If I don't like the way I'm treated, I'll go right back to New York, where I'm appreciated."

Paul Muni couldn't have done it better.

What a thrill—my name on a dressing room at Paramount Studios. It didn't even bother me that they wrote my name on the door in chalk. And a guy with a wet sponge kept walking up and down in front of it.

"Report to makeup."

I did as I was told, and I sat down in the makeup chair expecting to be glamorized. Wally Westmore, of the famous Westmore makeup family, gazed at my nose in disbelief.

He studied it straight on. He stood at the side, staring at its Rushmore proportions. He shook his head and walked to the other side. No better.

"We gotta do something about that nose," he said somberly.

"Like what?" I asked.

"Have you considered amputation?"

"Now wait a minute," I said indignantly. "I've had this nose for thirty-three years, and I've done all right with it. I want you to know I was a star on Broadway."

"In *Cyrano de Bergerac?*"

Wally went to work on my snoot. He darkened the flanges. He lightened the ski slope. I felt so self-conscious about my nose that I thought maybe Paramount was taking part in a Hire the Handicapped campaign.

Finally I got fed up and I said, "Enough with the makeup! You won't be able to camouflage this nose, so forget it. I'll just have to tell the public: Like me, like my nose."

20

Another problem: the eyes.

During my early days on *The Big Broadcast of 1938,* I felt uneasy. It was one thing to make three-day musical shorts. Appearing in a big-budget musical with a bevy of stars was something else.

The director, Mitchell Leisen, was a very sensitive man, and he understood my feelings. One day when I had a musical number to do with Shirley Ross, Mitch took me to lunch at Lucey's. Every studio had its nearby restaurant where actors and directors liked to go at lunchtime for a belt and a bit of relaxation from the day's shooting. Lucey's was the Paramount watering hole.

"Now, Bob," Mitch began, "there are some things you must learn about movie acting. The important thing is your eyes. When you're thinking about what you're going to say, you will alter the muscles of your eyes. All the great movie actors do that: they say their line with their eyes before they say it with their mouths. Garbo is the best example. She can be silent for twenty minutes, yet she will tell you the whole scene with her eyes.

"Remember that: think the emotion, and it will register in your eyes."

I went back to the set determined to follow his advice.

Shirley and I were going to do a song that Ralph Rainger and Leo Robin had written, "Thanks for the Memory." Mitch Leisen did something unusual with the song. Musical numbers were always prerecorded, then the singers synchronized their lip movements to the playback.

"I'm going to make a direct recording of this one," he announced. He had the full Paramount orchestra moved onto the set, and he ordered a slower pace to "Thanks for the Memory." Robin and Rainger argued that it was meant to be a fast song, but Mitch insisted on slowing it down.

Shirley and I went through the number. When it was over, Rainger and Robin were in tears. "We didn't realize the song was that good," one of them said.

I didn't realize how Mitch's lesson at Lucey's had sunk in. When I saw the rushes, I was astonished at my galloping orbs. I did everything with them except make them change places. Even today when I see the "Thanks for the Memory" number, I cringe.

One of the delights of *The Big Broadcast of 1938* was becoming acquainted with that rare comedy genius, W. C. Fields.

Sometimes established comedians aren't too happy about having younger comics in the same picture, but that wasn't the case with Bill Fields. Paul Jones, who turned out to be my producer and a good friend—the two didn't always go together—assured Fields that I was an okay guy, and that helped pave the way for a good relationship.

It was a delight to watch Fields up close and to observe some of the ways he operated. I learned that he had a habit of taking a script, analyzing it, and telling the Paramount bosses, "You know, I think I can fix this thing—for a price, of course." His price was $50,000.

For that fee, he would inject one or two of his old routines, some of them dating back to the *Follies* days.

Although I got along fine with Bill Fields, Mitch Leisen did not. That was only natural, since Fields was his own director. Mitch kept complaining that Bill was using old material, and even repeating himself.

One day Mitch really exploded. Fields was doing a boozing scene, and the director complained, "Mr. Fields, that's the same scene you did yesterday!"

"Not at all," Fields replied. "Yesterday I did the scene with a bottle of gin. Today I am doing it with a bottle of scotch."

Fields may have repeated himself, but I still found him to be an enormously inventive comic. I used to come on the set to watch him, even on days when I wasn't working. One day he was doing a scene in which the ocean liner had supposedly hit an iceberg.

The camera focused on Fields as he ad-libbed the action: "Women and children first! Women and children first! . . . Watch out—the little nippers are beating the ladies to the life-boats . . . Back, back, you little ba— bad children, you . . . Steady, everyone . . . Look—who's that? Why, the sailors are in the boats already. For shame! . . . And who's that in the water? The captain . . ." Fields continued on and on until finally he looked at the camera and said, "They're going to run out of film pretty soon."

Fields was naturally suspicious of strangers, but he accepted me into his confidence. I spent many hours in his dressing room, listening to his peculiar philosophy.

One day I was swapping stories with Fields when a distinguished-looking gentleman appeared at the dressing room door. I recognized him as one of the top brass in the Paramount hierarchy.

He introduced himself and said, "Mr. Fields, I am the chairman of the studio's Community Chest Drive. We're winding up our campaign, and you're one of the few remaining people we haven't had a response from. I'm sure it was an oversight, and you will want to contribute to help the community services for the poor, the orphaned, the widowed, and other unfortunates of Los Angeles.

"Very nice of you to drop by, my good man," Fields replied. "I'd like very much to help you with your highly admirable drive. Unfortunately, there is a very compelling reason why I cannot."

"What is that, Mr. Fields?" the executive asked.

"You see, I am a member of the FEBF."

The visitor looked puzzled. "The FEBF? I don't believe I'm familiar with that organization. What do the initials stand for?"

"—— Everybody But Fields."

W. C. Fields was one of many stars on the Paramount lot when I arrived in September of 1937. Even though I tried my hardest to be debonair, I couldn't help but be impressed by the galaxy. Look at who was under contract to Paramount at the time:

Actors: Edward Arnold, Lew Ayres, Benny Baker, George Barbier, Jack Benny, Charles Bickford, Ben Blue, Lee Bowman, William Boyd, Bob Burns, George Burns, Charles Butterworth, Gary Cooper, Buster Crabbe, Bing Crosby, Robert Cummings, Rufe Davis, Johnny Downs, James Ellison, W. C. Fields, William Frawley, Porter Hall, Russell Hayden, George (Gabby) Hayes, David Holt, Oscar Homolka, John Howard, Roscoe Karns, Billy Lee, Lucien Littlefield, Harold Lloyd, Fred MacMurray, Ray Middleton (both my buddies from *Roberta*), Ray Milland, Lloyd Nolan, Lynne Overman, Anthony Quinn, George Raft, Charlie Ruggles, Randolph Scott, Akim Tamiroff, and Warren William.

Actresses: Gracie Allen, Frances Dee, Marlene Dietrich, Frances Farmer, Franciska Gaal, Fay Holden, Marsha Hunt, Dorothy Lamour, Beatrice Lillie, Carole Lombard, Ida Lupino, Karen Morley, Gail Patrick, Elizabeth Patterson, Martha Raye, Shirley Ross, Gladys Swarthout, Virginia Weidler, and Mae West.

You can see why it was hard for me to maintain my cool in the company of such big names. Besides, there were lots of other stars who came to Paramount for single movies. One of them was really impressive—John Barrymore.

Even though he was then fighting a losing battle with the grape, Barrymore was still an impressive figure. Any newcomer to the acting profession like myself had to be in awe of his enormous

reputation. Imagine my thrill when I passed him on the street at Paramount and he nodded to me. The Great Profile recognizing the Ski Slope! It made my day.

I began to see Barrymore at NBC, too. He was there appearing on the Rudy Vallee show, and I did my Pepsodent show across the hall. When we passed, he would make a courtly bow and say, "How are you, Mr. Hope?" I would gulp and reply, "Fine. How are you, Mr. Barrymore?"

One day at NBC I was thrilled when he actually stopped to chat. "I understand that you're doing *Nothing but the Truth*," he remarked.

"Yes, sir, I am," I said.

"You know, I played that in the theatuh," he said. "In fact, I wrote it." I knew that wasn't true, but I went along with him. Then he added, "By the way, Mr. Hope, where are you making the picture?"

I was astonished. "I'm at Paramount!" I said. "The same studio where you're working. Don't you remember seeing me there?"

"Oh, that's right," he said. Then he pondered a moment and added, "Where *am* I?"

I gazed behind him at the man in the white suit who always accompanied him. The man gazed at me and shrugged.

Paramount was in a chance-taking mood in 1937, and the bosses decided to put me in another picture, *College Swing*. It was one of those light and airy comedy musicals that made no sense but a lot of dollars.

I had fun working with Martha Raye, Betty Grable, and George Burns and Gracie Allen, whom I had known in vaudeville. I also met two chaps who were to be important to me later. One was Jerry Colonna, a zany trombonist with eyes like organ stops and a mustache that quail could hide in. The other was E. C. Ennis, also known as Skinnay.

Skinnay had been singing with the Hal Kemp orchestra, and he had made a hit with his breathless style. One day I was playing golf with him, and he said, "You know, Bob, I'm puzzled. I don't know whether to stick with Hal's band or try starting my own."

"Gee, I think you ought to try it on your own, Skinnay," I said. "You've got a big following. I'll bet you could make it."

Skinnay did start his own band, and he made a success of it. Later when I was choosing a band for my radio show, I had to pick between Skinnay Ennis and Ozzie Nelson. Since I had ad-

College Swing
(with Martha Raye)

25

vised him to go into business for himself, I had to pick Skinnay. I wonder what ever happened to that Nelson fellow.

When I read the *College Swing* script, it seemed like a one-way ticket back to New York. I could have sent Paramount my lines on a pay telephone—and not exceeded the time limit. I realized that such a tiny part after *The Big Broadcast of 1938* would have been a comedown, and I wasn't ready to give up on my movie career—yet.

Luckily, the producer of *College Swing* was an old friend—Lewis Gensler, who had produced my first Broadway show, *Ballyhoo of 1932*. I pleaded with him, and he arranged to pad my part. Martha Raye and I did a comedy duet of a song that became a hit, "How'dja Like to Love Me?" It didn't hurt to be associated with two hit songs in my first two movies.

In fact, it was "Thanks for the Memory" that helped keep me on at Paramount. After *The Big Broadcast of 1938* was released, Damon Runyon devoted a full column to the song I did with Shirley Ross, saying it was the best thing he had seen in years. My press agent, Mack Millar, put a copy of the column on the desk of William LeBaron, the head of production at Paramount. My option was picked up for another picture.

Now my attitude toward Hollywood had changed from defiance to confidence. I was certain that Bob Hope was going to become a household name, like Bromo Seltzer or Sani-Flush.

Sometimes that confidence was shaken. Like one night when I made an appearance at the Biltmore Bowl with Mitch Leisen and Shirley Ross. Jimmy Grier was the orchestra leader and emcee at the Bowl, and he made a flowery introduction of Mitch as one of the screen's most distinguished directors. Then he came to Shirley and praised her beauty and talent.

"And with them is a young comedian from Broadway," Grier continued. "He stars with Miss Ross in *The Big Broadcast of 1938*, and you're going to be hearing a lot about him. How about a big hand for—BOB HOKE!"

You run into critics everywhere.

My next picture was *Give Me a Sailor*, which was made by the Harold Hurley unit. Harold was in charge of the low-budget pictures at Paramount, and I wasn't wild about becoming known as the King of the B's. But it was fun working with Martha Raye again, as well as Jack Whiting and a twenty-one-year-old blonde who was chiefly known as Jackie Coogan's bride—Betty Grable.

26

Give Me a Sailor
(with Martha Raye
and Jack Whiting)

Never Say Die

After *Give Me a Sailor*, it was option time again, and my fingernails were already bitten up to the elbow. By this time I was determined to stick it out in films. If Paramount wasn't smart enough to hold onto me, I'd give another studio a break.

My agents started shopping around, and they came up with an offer from Universal for $10,000 a picture, a bit of a comedown from the $20,000 I was getting at Paramount.

Walter Wanger agreed to hire me for a comedy called *Bedtime Story*. The only hurdle was Loretta Young, who had approval of her co-star.

"Wouldn't you like an actor who is young, suave, sophisticated, and charming?" my agent said.

"Yes," she replied. "David Niven."

And that's who she got, foolish girl.

Meanwhile my contract at Paramount was in the balance and could be tipped either way. "Thanks for the Memory" turned out to be my good-luck piece. The song had become a big hit, and Paramount was looking for a way to cash in on it.

George Bagnall, one of the executives at Paramount, came up with the solution: "We've got a property called *Up Pops the Devil*. It pretty much follows the lyrics of 'Thanks for the Memory.' Why not change the title to *Thanks for the Memory* and star Bob Hope and Shirley Ross in it?"

"Not a bad idea," said Bill LeBaron. "We ought to be able to make it inexpensively, say in the neighborhood of two hundred thousand."

I was playing in the same neighborhood for my next two pictures, *Never Say Die* and *Some Like It Hot,* and I feared I would never graduate to the high-rent district.

Some Like It Hot was the rock-bottom point in my movie career. After that one, there was no place to go but up. For years afterward, Bing wouldn't let me forget it. Whenever I started to give him the needle about something, he came back with a rejoinder, something like, "By the way, can you come over to the house tonight, Bob? We're going to barbecue some steaks and then all sit down and watch *Some Like It Hot*." That shut me up in a hurry.

I thought perhaps I was wrong about *Some Like It Hot* when I saw the preview. Some of my screaming fans picked me up on their shoulders and started rushing me toward the stage. I happened to be in the balcony at the time.

It was radio that saved me from Harold Hurley's B-hive.

My radio career had been as spotty as a leopards' reunion. I had been on the air for Bromo Seltzer ("America's Headache," was the billing) and for Atlantic Refining ("America's Refined Comedian"). I was on the Woodbury Soap show ("America's Cleanest Comedian"?) when I moved West. The rest of the show came from New York, but I was piped in from Hollywood. That presented a problem.

My part of the show amounted to only five minutes. I couldn't very well deliver my clever jokes to an empty studio. Nor was there much chance of inducing an audience to sit down for a five-minute show.

I scouted around the NBC studios and discovered that the Edgar Bergen and Charlie McCarthy show immediately preceded the Woodbury broadcast. Both Edgar and his blockheaded partner were friends of mine. They had been in *Ziegfeld Follies* with me, but had been dropped from the show because of overlength. Now they were the biggest stars in radio.

Why not borrow Edgar's audience? I arranged with the NBC ushers to channel the unsuspecting guests out of the Bergen studio and into mine. The people laughed so hard at my jokes they didn't even mind being chained to the seats.

When the next radio season rolled around, I was appearing on the Lucky Strike show with Dick Powell as emcee. At least I didn't have to corral my own audience. But I longed for my own show, so I could call the shots and not merely come on and tell a few dozen jokes.

The chance came in the fall of 1938. Lord & Thomas, the advertising agency, was looking for a replacement for Amos 'n' Andy. The sponsor was Pepsodent Toothpaste. I flashed my pearlies and got the job.

This time I was determined to succeed. I felt that I hadn't paid enough attention to my material on the previous shows, and that's why I didn't last. I set about to find the best comedy writers, not just the vaudeville old-timers who were writing most of the other radio shows. I wanted fresh young talent, newcomers who were willing to submit wild and wacky comedy.

Among the youngsters who wrote for me in those early shows: Al Schwartz, Norman Sullivan, Milt Josefsberg, Jack Rose, Mel Shavelson, Jack Douglas, Norman Panama, Mel Frank, Sherwood Schwartz. They have become famous producers, directors, and

TWO SLEEPY PEOPLE

Words by FRANK LOESSER   Music by HOAGY CARMICHAEL

le suggested by LYNN GARLAND

Adolph Zukor presents

'Thanks for the Memory'

with

Bob Hope • Shirley Ross

A Paramount Picture

FAMOUS MUSIC CORPORATION • 1619 B'way.   New York

writers. Norman Sullivan deserves some kind of Carnegie medal for bravery above and beyond the call of gag writing—he's still working for me.

In those years, every radio show had its own theme song. The advertising minds came up with one for me: "Wintergreen for President," from *Of Thee I Sing.* It was to be sung to the lines: "Hope is Here for Pepsodent."

It sounded all right to me, but then I was told that the copyright owners demanded $250 for each use of the song.

"Nuts to that," I said. "I know a song that we can get much cheaper, and it'll be better. It's that one I sang in *The Big Broadcast of 1938.*"

And that's how "Thanks for the Memory" got tagged to my name forever.

The Pepsodent show began on Tuesday night, September 27, 1938. I'd like to say it was an immediate hit. But I'd be lying.

The truth is that it took four or five weeks to develop a format. At first the show was just a collection of jokes and routines. Then we developed the formula of using guest stars and the show's regulars to follow a story line. That held the audience's interest much better.

The important thing was material. I was editing the jokes with a careful hand and encouraging the young writers to let their imaginations fly. They did.

Everything worked for us. Skinnay Ennis was the bandleader, and his thinness provided a variety of jokes. Jerry Colonna contributed his zanyisms. Jerry, like many swing musicians, had the habit of calling everyone "Gate." On the fifth show of the first season, we had a sketch in which Jer played a doctor; it was supposed to be a takeoff on Bing's current movie, *Dr. Rhythm.* Jer made his entrance with the line "Greetings, Gate, let's operate!"

The audience roared. None of us could really understand the immense reaction, but on every show thereafter Jer entered with a saying that rhymed with "Greetings, Gate." Soon everybody in the country was saying it.

Then we ran a contest to name the baby of our announcer, Bill Goodwin. I think it was Jack Douglas who was entranced with the name of the violin prodigy Yehudi Menuhin. On one show Colonna suggested naming the baby Yehudi. Again the audience was convulsed. "Who's Yehudi?" became a song and a national phrase.

In the following season, we introduced Brenda and Cobina, two man-chasing chicks who had all the glamour of lady wrestlers. In that same season the Pepsodent show featured a teen-age singer by the name of Judy Garland. She was great in all departments, from belting over a song to socking over comedy lines.

Judy delivered one of the biggest laugh lines we had in that second—or any—season. The scripts had established that Judy had a schoolgirl crush on me—now is that so hard to imagine? I was always talking about the beauty of Madeleine Carroll, and I promised that she would appear on the show.

Two or three weeks of build-up went by, and finally Madeleine Carroll appeared. I had been impressing on the show's cast to be respectful to Miss Carroll. Finally, I had to introduce her to Judy.

Judy immediately contemplated Madeleine's blond locks and said, "Hmmmm . . . peroxide." I never heard an audience laugh so long.

We were doing some wild comedy on the radio show, and many of the punch lines were repeated all across the country. Most of them were spoken by Jerry Colonna: "Okay, so I ain't neat!" "You and your education!" "That's what I keep telling them down at the office!" "Give me a drag on that before you throw it away."

If you can remember those lines, you're a lot older than you admit.

The Pepsodent show was catching on—fast. So fast that even my Paramount bosses were impressed. They began to take another look at the chap who was making those B pictures with Martha Raye and Shirley Ross.

Some Like It Hot
(with Rufe Davis)

The Cat and the Canary was the turning point for my movie career.

Paramount apparently got the message about my radio show and decided to put me in an A picture tailored for me. Before then, I was wearing other actors' castoffs—and sometimes the patches were showing.

I was thrilled to have Paulette Goddard as my leading lady. Not only was she beautiful and talented; she was also the leading lady—and wife—of my earliest idol, Charlie Chaplin.

Paulette was a little nervous working with another comedian, but we got along fine. One day I ran into her at the Santa Anita race track, and she said casually, "You know Charles, don't you?"

I gulped. There in front of me was the legend. Twenty years before, I had imitated him in front of the firehouse in Cleveland.

31

The Cat and the Canary
(with Paulette Goddard)

Once in New York, I had waited on the street an hour and a half just to catch a glimpse of him; a friend had told me, "That's Charlie Chaplin's car—he's inside that restaurant."

Now I was meeting the great man, and I tried to utter something that made sense. I don't think I succeeded.

"Young man," he said, "I've been watching the rushes of *The Cat and the Canary* every night. I want you to know that you are one of the best timers of comedy I've ever seen."

Right away he put me at ease—and in the clouds.

After *The Cat and the Canary*, Paramount told me to hit the road.

"You can't do this to me!" I protested. "*The Cat and the Canary* was a hit, wasn't it?"

32

"Now, relax, Bob. We're trying to tell you that you're going to do a picture called *The Road to Singapore* with Bing Crosby and Dorothy Lamour."

"Yeah, but that doesn't give you the right to drop my option— you what?"

It took a brief period for the news to sink in. What a break to be working with two of the biggest stars in Hollywood!

I had known Bing for about seven years. We had met on Forty-eighth Street near the Friars Club in New York in 1932. Two months later, we were appearing on the same bill together at the Capitol Theater on Broadway. Bing had made several movies and was appearing on his own radio show for Cremo cigars, but he was extremely cordial to a peasant out of vaudeville. In fact, we worked up some routines together to delight the Capitol audiences.

One of the routines was an old vaudeville standby about two persons meeting on the street.

"Two farmers meeting each other on the street." We approached each other from opposite sides of the stage, then I pointed my thumbs downward and Bing milked them.

"Two politicians meeting each other on the street." We hailed each other, then started picking each other's pockets.

Bing and I renewed our acquaintance after I came to Paramount. He and Pat O'Brien were operating the Del Mar race track, and on the night the track opened for the season they staged an entertainment for the guests from Hollywood.

"Why don't you and I do some of those routines we did at the Capitol?" Bing suggested.

"Sure thing," I said. I was never shy about accepting engagements—then or now.

Bing and I did our thing, and the audience loved it. Especially Bill LeBaron, who was the production boss at Paramount.

"Those two boys work well together," Bill said, not realizing that we'd had a rehearsal seven years before. "We ought to put them in a picture together."

It wasn't hard to find a property. Paramount had an old script that had been written for George Burns and Gracie Allen. They were unavailable, so it was rebuilt for Jack Oakie and Fred Mac-Murray. That didn't work out, either, so the picture was handed to Bing and me—and Dotty.

I had known Dorothy Lamour, too. When I was in Broadway shows, I formed the habit of going for a midnight walk just to un-

SWEET POTATO PIPER

Lyric by
JOHNNY BURKE
a.s.c.a.p.

Music by
JAMES V. MONACO
a.s.c.a.p.

BING CROSBY
The ROAD TO SINGAPORE
DOROTHY   BOB
LAMOUR · HOPE

SANTLY-JOY-SELECT, INC. · 1619 BROADWAY · N. Y. C.

wind and get some exercise—that was when it was safe to take a walk in New York. It's a habit I've never been able to kick, and you can still find me doing the Harry Truman bit in the early yawning hours on the streets of North Hollywood or wherever else I'm stopping over. On one of my New York strolls I stopped at a night spot called One Fifth Avenue.

I was glad I did. I saw and heard a beautiful chantootsie with a sultry voice. Her name was Dorothy Lamour. Sometimes I reminisce about it with Dotty, and I tell her I threw my first nickel at her.

"You mean your second nickel," she says. "You bought a pocketbook with your first nickel." The nerve of that girl!

Later she was singing at the Navarre Club on Central Park South, and I dropped in to hear her sing and have a chat. She went on to Hollywood and did more for a piece of cloth than any American woman since Betsy Ross. It was called a sarong.

I was delighted when I found that Dorothy Lamour was in my first Hollywood movie, *The Big Broadcast of 1938*. I was thrilled when I thought I might get the girl in *The Road to Singapore*. But the cards were as well stacked as she was.

"*You* get *Lamour?*" the producer said. "Really, Mr. Hope, we're trying to make a comedy, not a fantasy."

During *The Road to Singapore*, Bing and I developed the system which helped contribute to the success of the *Roads*. He and I had appeared on each other's radio shows, and our writers had developed an easygoing, semi-insulting give-and-take between us. We carried that over into the picture.

Our radio writers supplied us with lines. Bing and I would go into a scene and start tossing the gags back and forth, much to the surprise of everyone. Including our director, Victor Schertzinger. But he saw that it was working, and he let us go ahead.

"You know, I really shouldn't take money for this job," he confessed one day. "All I do is say 'stop' and 'go.'"

He was delighted, but the movie script writers weren't. They were two fine writers: Frank Butler and Don Hartman, and they resented having Bing and me tamper with their script. Frank used to come on the set and scowl; that only made us needle him.

"Hey, Frank!" I yelled to him before a scene began. "If you hear anything that sounds like one of your lines, just yell 'Bingo!'"

The Crosby-Hope system was tough on Dotty Lamour. She studied her script like the good pro she is; then she got in a scene

34

with Bing and me, and she didn't hear anything she could recognize. She felt like the judge at a tennis match.

During one long scene she finally exclaimed, "Hey, boys—will you please let me get my line in?"

The system worked. The *Road* pictures had the excitement of a live entertainment, not a movie set. Crew workers at Paramount fought to be assigned to a *Road,* because they knew it would be a ball. Some stars banned visitors, but Bing and I liked to have people around. New visitors sparked new gags. Sometimes Bing and I yelled back and forth between our dressing rooms to try out new material.

The Road to Singapore (with Dorothy Lamour and Bing Crosby)

Vic Schertzinger was the ideal director for our technique. I remember one scene we were doing with Dotty, Bing, and myself on Stage 5. In those days, most directors would film a master shot taking in the whole scene, then move closer for a medium shot, then shoot each principal actor in close-ups. Later the scene would be cut together with various angles.

We did a scene that lasted about five minutes, with Bing and me throwing barbs back and forth and Dotty trying to get a word in.

"Cut and print!" Vic said. "Let's go to the next setup."

The assistant director, Dink Templeton, drew Vic aside and said quietly, "Vic, didn't you notice that Bob stepped out of his light for a minute?"

"Yes, I noticed," the director replied.

"But don't you want to make another shot—or get some other angles for protection?" the assistant asked.

"No," Vic said. "That scene was like a piece of music; it was well orchestrated and it flowed beautifully. Maybe the flutes were off-key or the cellos didn't come in at the right time. But the total performance was great. I could shoot that scene again, but the actors wouldn't have the same spark they had the first time. And if I made a lot of protection shots, the producers would find some way to foul up the scene in the cutting room. Next setup."

As my movie career started to develop momentum, I developed a mode of operation which has continued through the years. Whenever I received a movie script, I handed it to my gag writers. They submitted jokes to punch up scenes in the picture.

There was nothing new in this. All of the notable comics in films had retained gag men. I was employing some of the best comedy minds in the business. So why not use them in pictures as well as radio (and later, television)?

This practice wasn't always popular with directors and script writers. But usually they realized that the more laughs, the better the picture. And many a time my writers provided lines that lifted a scene out of the ordinary.

Gag writers are a strange, bright, exhilarating, exasperating breed. I should know. I sometimes spend more time with them than I do with my family—or so my family tells me. I believe I was the first of the comedians to hire several writers at a time. I think maybe I was also the first to admit openly that I employed writers. In the early days of radio, comedians fostered the illusion that all of those funny sayings came right out of their own skulls.

Ed Wynn had a brilliant gag man who wasn't allowed to come to the radio studio; he had to remain a silent partner, and unseen, too.

In my own early days in radio, I used to labor over my scripts with my writer, Wilkie Mahoney. We worked together every night until the early yawning hours. But I found out I couldn't maintain that kind of a schedule and keep up my performing career, too. When you're writing, you need time to think and grope. With my career going in all directions, I had to make an appointment to brush my teeth.

So I called in help. At one time on the Pepsodent show, because of overlapping options, I had thirteen comedy writers on the payroll. "Here comes Hope's army," they used to say around NBC.

We even made jokes about it on the radio show. Once I summoned the writers to a script meeting, and Judy Garland cracked on the air: "It looks like Notre Dame coming out for the second half."

I'd like to say that my writers have always been respectful, obedient, and courteous to me. I'd like to say that, but nobody would believe me. Especially the writers.

The essence of comedy is give-and-take. Sometimes I take more than I give. You'd be astonished at some of the things those guys say about me.

Wilkie Mahoney worked with me for many years. "I knew Bob when he only had a hundred thousand dollars," Wilkie says. "Now he's got engraved idiot cards."

Once I hired a young writer named Bert Styles for thirteen weeks before the summer hiatus. Bert was new in town and he asked one of the old writers, Norman Sullivan, "What does Bob do about summer?"

"Oh, he lets it come," Norman replied.

The writers are always practicing one-upmanship on me, trying to pull gags that will stop me cold. But two can play that game.

During the early years of radio, the writers and I often worked late at night on scripts. Along about midnight, I would get a craving for ice cream. I wasn't pregnant or anything; I just like ice cream late at night.

The job of fetching the ice cream always went to the youngest member of the writing staff, and in those prewar years it was Sherwood Schwartz. Then Sherwood got drafted.

During the war, we were broadcasting from New York one

week, and Sherwood happened to be in the city on furlough. "Let's play a gag on Bob," the writers said.

At ten o'clock that night, the writers and I were agonizing over the radio script in my hotel room. A knock came at the door. It was Sherwood Schwartz in uniform, carrying a pint of ice cream. I hadn't seen him in a year, but I wasn't going to let the writers have their sport. "I hope it's vanilla," I said.

You have to be quick on your feet to avoid the needle from those boys. Once we did the Christmas show in Alaska, and I gave an interview saying that I lost money by traveling to far-off places for shows (it's still true).

When I arrived at NBC for a script session, the writers had put out milk cartons filled with coins, with signs reading, "Help Poor Old Bob."

I didn't flinch. "All right, you guys," I said, "who's the s.o.b. who put slugs in here?"

Over the years, the majority of my writers have been Jewish, and that evokes some laughs, too. Once I was going out to lunch with the writers and as we passed in front of NBC, I pointed across the street.

"See that synagogue over there?" I said. "I just bought the property."

"There goes our last place to hide," muttered Mort Lachman.

Nothing and nobody escape the barbs of the writers, not even my own family. It's no secret that my wife Dolores is a devout Catholic. One day I was meeting her at the airport, and I took along one of the writers, Charlie Lee. When Dolores got off the plane, there were a couple of priests in front of her and three nuns behind her.

"Why can't she take out regular insurance, like everybody else?" Charlie cracked.

Whenever comedy writers meet, the conversation often gets around to Barney Dean. He was the gag man's gag man.

Barney was sort of a good-luck piece for me. In fact, he was almost small enough to hang on my watch chain.

He was five feet one, bald, and had a face that even his mother must have had doubts about loving. But inside he was pure gold. He was also one of the funniest men alive.

Barney had little confidence in himself. Once he gave a watch to Buddy DeSylva, who was then head of production at Paramount. Engraved on the back of the watch was: "To Buddy, this is a lot of crap, but when you don't have any talent, you have to do these things, Barney."

The truth is he was loaded with talent, as a funnyman and as a friend.

I first became acquainted with Barney in Chicago in 1928. Barney and his brother Sid were doing a dance act at the Stratford Theater, and I was on the bill as emcee. Barney was a good friend of Charlie Hogan, booker for the Stratford.

"How is Hope doing?" Charlie asked.

"He is sensational," Barney replied. His endorsement helped me stretch a one-week stand to six months, and I've been working steadily ever since.

I didn't see much of Barney in the years afterward, but I kept hearing stories about him. Most gag writers knew him, and they traded his latest cracks. One day I was working with the writers at NBC and Barney dropped in.

"What have you been doing, Barney?" I asked.

He shrugged. "Same old thing—selling handcuffs."

For some reason—maybe because he was so loath to sell himself—Barney was unemployed most of the time. When Bing and I were making *The Road to Singapore,* Barney came on the set selling Christmas cards.

"You know," I said to Bing, "Barney's a very funny guy."

"He sure is," Bing replied. "I know all about him."

"It's too bad we can't get him a job on this picture."

Bing called the assistant director. "Put Barney Dean on the payroll as a writer on this picture," Bing said.

Barney went to work immediately. He never really wrote anything. He stayed on the set at all times and watched rehearsals. Before the take, Barney would say to Bing or me: "Wouldn't it be funnier if you said this . . ." More often than not, he would come up with an inspired bit of dialogue. Or if the scene stank, he wasn't afraid to tell us.

Sometimes I liked to tease him. He'd say, "How about this line . . ." I'd listen to the joke with a straight face and reply, "That's funny?"

"Where are my dancing shoes?" Barney would wail.

Both Bing and I found Barney extremely useful, and great fun to have around, too. His cheerfulness and bright humor made the long day's shooting go much faster. Bing and I always insisted on having him assigned to our pictures. Finally Buddy DeSylva said, "As long as you're going to keep Barney working, we might as

The Ghost Breakers
(with Paulette Goddard
and Anthony Quinn)

well put him under contract." I had my agents negotiate a deal that brought Barney $500 a week from Paramount.

During the war, Barney accompanied me on overseas trips, even though he thought flying was strictly for the birds. Again, I tormented him: "Don't worry, Barney, these guys know how to fly this thing. So there's a little oil leak coming out of the engine. It doesn't mean a thing."

All Barney could say was, "Yeahhhhh."

On one trans-Pacific flight, the plane did a lot of bouncing, and Barney turned chartreuse. He was reeling when he finally stepped onto land at Midway Island. "You mean to tell me that Phil Harris feels this way every morning?" he said.

Once on a flight from Brisbane to Sydney, our plane got in real trouble. I tried to convince Barney of the danger, but he thought I was kidding him again. "Bob, leave me alone," he said.

I practically dragged him to the bomber's blister and showed him the feathered propeller. "That thing is supposed to be going around," I told him.

Barney looked at the motionless propeller and said, "Yeahhhhhh!"

Now he was really scared. He became more so when he saw our luggage, cases of liquor and cigarettes being jettisoned. When we landed safely, Barney muttered, "Thank God! I thought I was going to be thrown over next."

One day Barney heard that Bing was going to New York. "Say, Bing," he said, "would you do me a favor?"

"Sure, Barney, what is it?" Bing said.

"When you get to New York, would you go up to 127th Street and see my mother? You have to climb five flights of stairs, then just knock on the door and say hello and give her five thousand dollars."

One of my favorite stories about Barney concerned the night he decided to take a little walk in Beverly Hills. The Beverly Hills police are famous for stopping people who walk on the streets at night. It's such a strange sight to see folks walking in California that the cops get suspicious.

Barney was strolling down Camden Drive when a motorcycle policeman pulled up beside him. Barney put on his most innocent face and asked, "How fast was I going?"

Barney could find humor in anything, even death. Once Louie Shurr was seriously ill, and everyone was concerned about whether he'd pull through (he did). Barney ran into Bullets Durgom, an agent who was built just like Barney and Louie—about five feet one. Between the three of them, they could have supported a West Coast franchise of Adler Elevators.

"Did you hear about Louie being sick?" Bullets asked.

"Yes, I'm watching him very closely," Barney replied. "I get his shoes."

One day in 1950 at rehearsal for the radio show, Barney complained of being sick. I suggested that he should go to a hospital, and my radio agent, Jimmy Saphier, drove him to St. Joseph's in Burbank. Barney refused to take it seriously. "Jimmy, you'd better take my wallet," he said. "I don't want these nuns rolling me."

Barney left the hospital after a brief stay, but he still didn't seem well. He was the kind of guy who would be concerned if you sneezed, but he never showed any concern for his own health. One day he told me, "I'm going into the hospital for an ulcer on Thursday; I'll be out on Friday."

He never made it. The doctor told me it was cancer, and Barney had forty-eight hours to live. When I went to see him at the hospital that night, I wondered if he knew.

Al Jolson had died a few weeks before. When Barney saw me, he grinned and said, "Got any messages for Joley?"

After *The Road to Singapore*, Paramount no longer chalked my name on the dressing room door. Now they used washable ink. I did another thriller with Paulette Goddard, *The Ghost Breakers*, with George Marshall as director. Over the years I've done six other movies with George, and I found him to be an amazing guy. He was in films before D. W. Griffith owned his first Brownie, and he continued making movies more than sixty years!

I guess I was doing okay at the box office, because Paramount released four of my pictures in 1941.

Caught in the Draft was a title that Buddy DeSylva dreamed up. With the draft starting in America, it was a great title, but Buddy had no script. He brought Harry Tugend over from Fox to do an original screenplay about a movie star who gets drafted. It was the first of many films I made with Harry. I played the romantic movie star. I guess Paramount wanted to see just how good an actor I was.

Caught in the Draft was also my first movie with David Butler. Old Blubberbutt, as I irreverently called him, was another veteran of silent comedy, and he was a delight to work with. He set the tone for the picture on the first day of shooting. We were

Caught in the Draft

Caught in the Draft
(with Eddie Bracken
and Lynne Overman)

doing a battle scene, and as Dave was giving instructions, he disappeared into a shell hole. I don't know whether he was purposely trying for laughs, but he certainly got them. Everything was free and easy on the picture after that.

Well, almost.

On the very last day of shooting, the script called for a scene at "dusk." That's always a tough shot to film, because the light disappears fast. We were out in Malibu Canyon at the army camp that had been built for the picture. Since there was a delay until the sun started to set, I decided to go for a ride with Harry Ray, my makeup man. I came across a beautiful canyon, and I stopped to take in the sight.

Meanwhile, back at the ranch, Dave Butler was steaming. The sun was beginning to drop behind the Malibu mountains, and no Hope. He finally shot the scene with a double.

In the middle of my reverie over nature's beauty, I suddenly realized that I was needed on the set. Harry and I raced back to the location and found the crew packing up to leave. Dave Butler's bounteous belly was shaking with rage. But instead of bawling me out, he directed his anger at Harry Ray: "At least I thought that *you* would have enough brains to get back on time!" Meaning that I didn't.

Oh yes, there was a sequel to the story. Later I bought the canyon.

Caught in the Draft is a pleasant memory for a very special reason. It was released at the time when England was fighting alone against the air attacks of Nazi Germany. Walter Winchell reported in his column that the homeless of Coventry gathered in the bombed-out cathedral to watch a showing of *Caught in the Draft*, and it increased their spirits greatly. And Quentin Reynolds said that the picture played around the clock in a London theater, with crowds at every performance. It felt good to be able to help the morale of my native country.

Bing, Dotty, and I hit the *Road* again in 1941, this time to *Zanzibar*. Again our tour director was Vic Schertzinger. My other releases that year were *Nothing but the Truth*, directed by Elliott Nugent, with whom I did four other films; and *Louisiana Purchase*, based on the Broadway hit. The director was Irving Cummings, who had been a silent-film star.

Irving was one of the old-style directors with a flair, and I loved to hear him intone "Lights! Camera! Action!" He could make it sound like a soliloquy from Shakespeare.

One day we were doing a water scene. To get a shimmering effect, Irving had assigned workers to move the water with small paddles. I'll never forget how he started the scene that day: "Lights! Camera! Start your agitators!"

From my radio monologues of 1941:
"Madeleine Carroll and I are making a picture called *My Favorite Blonde*. She's a spy, and she keeps chasing me. That's right, Madeleine Carroll keeps chasing me . . . And you think Walt Disney makes fantastic pictures! . . .

"Madeleine Carroll . . . Yes, sir . . . I guess I'm the only man in the country right now who wants longer working hours . . .

"This morning the producer asked me to study my lines . . . I'm working on a picture with Madeleine Carroll, and he wants me to study *my* lines! . . .

"They gave Madeleine her choice of three leading men, and she chose me . . . Boy, did the others get sore! . . . In fact, Donald Duck, Dumbo, and I still aren't on speaking terms!"

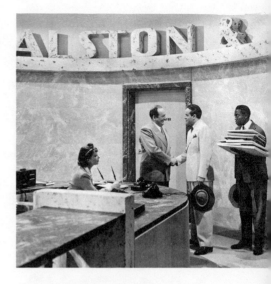

Nothing but the Truth
(with Edward Arnold and Willie Best)

Louisiana Purchase
(with Victor Moore)

As you can see, my writers had a field day when I appeared in *My Favorite Blonde* with Madeleine Carroll. It was a real thrill for me, too, and it might not have happened if I hadn't opened my big mouth—many times.

Like many another red-blooded American male, I thought Madeleine Carroll was the epitome of beauty. And I had said so many times on my radio show, so that it got to be a running gag. One day she telephoned me.

"Bob, I want to thank you for all that wonderful publicity you've given me on your radio show," she said. "You know, we ought to do a picture together."

A movie with Madeleine Carroll! It seemed as impossible as flying to the moon. (That was before flying to the moon was possible.) She was the queen of the Paramount lot, a regal beauty from England who was also a fine actress.

To my surprise, Paramount didn't think it was such a bad idea for me to co-star with Madeleine. In fact, it was a toss-up between Charles Boyer and me. But they chose me because I had more charm, more *savoir-faire*, more stock in Paramount.

My Favorite Blonde points out an important lesson: always be nice to your writers and someday they may be nice to you.

The original story for *My Favorite Blonde* was written by two lads named Norman Panama and Mel Frank. I had given them their first jobs as comedy writers when I started the Pepsodent show in 1938.

They were a couple of college kids from Chicago who came to Hollywood to break into show business. I was always on the look-out for fresh talent, and I asked them to submit some material. They sent me forty-seven single-spaced pages of jokes. I asked them to come and see me at Paramount.

"Hey—I've been enjoying you guys all night," I told them. "I want you to be with me."

I asked Mel and Norm to sign for seven years, but they were too crafty for that. They signed on for a year, and their first assignment was to write a guest shot for Groucho Marx. "Go see Groucho," I told them, "but don't suggest any jokes. *He's* the comedian."

Panama and Frank decided they weren't going to leave their first assignment to chance. Back in Chicago, they had written a play about a Depression family raising rabbits. They had a thousand jokes about rabbits. So they told Groucho: "Hope has the idea that you have a rabbit farm and you try to sell it to him."

My Favorite Blonde
(with Madeleine Carroll)

They came back to me and said, "Groucho has an idea that he owns a rabbit farm and tries to sell it to you." That's how they unloaded all their rabbit jokes.

After a year on my show, Panama and Frank left me to work for another comedian, the cowards. When the job folded, they wrote an original treatment for a movie designed for Madeleine Carroll and me. They called it *Snowball in Hell*. Which gives you an idea of the chances they thought I had with her. Later the title was changed to *My Favorite Blonde*.

Only one thing worried me about *My Favorite Blonde*. Sidney Lanfield was assigned to direct, and he had a reputation for being tough with actors. I expressed my doubts to Buddy DeSylva.

45

The Road to Zanzibar
(with Dorothy Lamour
and Bing Crosby)

"Look, Bob," said Buddy, "in this business you're going to encounter a certain amount of heels. You'll just have to learn to put up with them."

My fears proved unfounded. Sidney Lanfield turned out to be a pussycat. We got along so beautifully that we did four more pictures together.

Like Webster's dictionary,
We're Morocco-bound . . .

Ah yes, in 1942, Bing, Dotty, and I were off on our merry adventures again. As in the first *Road,* Tony Quinn was the heavy—

this was long before Zorba the Greek had opened up his first restaurant. Directing *The Road to Morocco*—the three Bs. No, not Bach, Beethoven, and Brahms, but Blubberbutt Butler.

Dave was a cagey character. He knew that Bing and I spent half our studio time on the phone, talking about our radio shows, our investments, and other minor matters. Dave wanted our full attention. In those days there was only one telephone on a movie set; not even the biggest star had a phone in his dressing room. So Dave ordered the assistant director to station the phone for *The Road to Morocco* a block and a half away from the set where we were working.

Not only that. The telephone was installed under a pile of lumber, so that anyone answering it would have to slide in horizontally to pick up the receiver.

Dave's answer to AT&T worked well until the day that Sam Goldwyn called. It came at a time when Dave was directing a crowd scene that involved a couple of hundred mules and twice that many people.

"Mr. Goldwyn is calling you, Mr. Butler," the assistant director said.

Dave told Bing and me and the entire company to wait, then he trudged across the sound stage and into the next one and slid under the lumber pile. "Hello, Sam. What is it?" Dave said.

Goldwyn was working on the script that Dave was going to direct next—for me, as it turned out. For fifteen minutes, Goldwyn expounded on the intricacies of the story while the *Road to Morocco* company waited. Finally Goldwyn said, "Thanks very much for calling me," and hung up.

We had a lot of adventures on *The Road to Morocco*, and some of them were in the script. The real ones were lots of fun—it says here.

Like the time Bing and I were washed up on the North African coast. A camel sneaks up behind us and licks us on the cheeks. We begin to think it's love at second sight until we see that it was a camel doing the kissing, not each other.

I don't know if you've ever been kissed by a camel, but I've got to tell you that it's not like being kissed by Raquel Welch. This particular camel may have been listening to my radio show, because after he kissed me, he spat right in my face.

You wouldn't believe what a camel stores up in his chaw. I thought I had been hit by the Casbah Garbage Department.

When you see *The Road to Morocco* on the late show, you'll

47

The Road to Utopia
(with Bing Crosby, before the fall)

notice that I stagger out of the scene when the camel spits at me. Bing broke up, and I was gasping for breath, but Dave kept the camera rolling.

"Great scene," he said afterward.

"But don't you want another take?" I said, wiping the muck out of my eyes. "The whole crew was laughing, and I disappeared out of the frame."

"No, that's it," Dave replied. For years afterward, people asked him, "How did you get that camel to spit at Hope on cue?" Dave replied, "I worked with that beast for weeks until it responded to my direction."

Dave was full of tricks. During one scene in *The Road to Morocco*, Bing and I were to be chased through the Casbah by Arabian horsemen. Dave had hired an old pal to lead the stunt riders—Ken Maynard, the cowboy star.

I guess Ken was trying to make a show of it. Because when Dave gave the cue, Ken led his horsemen through the Casbah like the first furlong of the Kentucky Derby.

"My God, Paramount wants to get rid of us!" I yelled as I saw the horses charging at me.

"We never should have asked for a raise," Bing agreed. He made a flying dive, and I jumped off the set, landing on the concrete floor.

"Cut!" Dave yelled. "Great shot!"

"Great shot!" Bing replied. "You almost killed Bob and me!"

"Oh, I wouldn't do that," Dave said. "Not until the final scene, anyway."

That wasn't the first time that I learned movies could be a risky business. In my first picture, *The Big Broadcast of 1938*, there was a running gag that Martha Raye would break mirrors every time she looked into them. For one shipboard scene, she was supposed to look into a room-length mirror and the thing would crack.

A funny scene, but it almost turned into a tragedy. The special-effects men put too much air pressure behind the mirror. When Martha looked into it, the huge mirror shattered with the noise of a cannon, and thousands of glass fragments were blasted toward us. It was a miracle that no one was seriously hurt.

Several years later, Bing and I were making *The Road to Utopia*. One of the scenes called for Bing and me to bed down in our Klondike cabin and be joined by a bear. A real bear. They told us it was a very tame bear, but Bing and I had our doubts.

48

We climbed under a rug and feigned sleep. The bear came sniffing up to us. Then we heard a growl. Right then I had laundry problems.

"Did you hear what I heard?" Bing asked.

"I sure did," I said. "Lead the way, Dad."

We set an Olympic record for leaping out of bed—Errol Flynn couldn't have done it faster.

"That's it with the bear," Bing announced, and I heartily agreed. The next day, the same bear tore an arm off his trainer.

One day on *Utopia*, we were shooting a glacier scene on the De Mille stage—named after Cecil B. because he shot many of his epics there. Bing and I were supposed to be climbing a wall of ice, and we were doing it many feet above the stage floor. Or-

The Road to Morocco
(with Dorothy Lamour)

dinarily there were mattresses beneath us, but somebody moved them.

Right in the middle of the scene the rope broke, and Bing and I went tumbling down. I looked for a soft spot to land and found it: Crosby. His back hasn't been the same since.

Over the years, I have been subjected to many more indignities, all for the sake of Art. If I ever catch him, I'm going to kill the guy.

My movie career was progressing nicely in the early 1940s, but my salary wasn't. I realized that when I went to Chicago for a personal appearance. I had never seen such crowds, not even at the World Series. I sent for my agent, Doc Shurr. He came from California, saw the crowds, and agreed that perhaps I was being underpaid by Paramount.

Doc went to see Y. Frank Freeman, who was then the business boss of Paramount. Freeman was a drawling Georgia gentleman —the Y. stood for "Y'all"—and he did business by the letter.

"Ah won' do anythin' foh Hope until he lives up to his contract," Freeman said.

Doc Shurr had another idea. Paramount had just borrowed Gary Cooper from Samuel Goldwyn. The Doctor reasoned that we could get Paramount to loan me to Goldwyn, who had been wanting me to do a picture for him. Then we could ask for more money than Paramount was paying me.

You've probably heard about Sam Goldwyn and his Goldwynisms . . . "A verbal contract isn't worth the paper it's written on" . . . "Anybody who sees a psychiatrist should have his head examined" . . . Sam may have said such things, because he had a way of mangling the English language. But when it came to business, he was as shrewd as a Yankee trader.

Doc Shurr and his partner, Al Melnick, went to see Sam about making a deal. Sam began by saying what a great comedian I was, how eager he was to make a picture with me, and how everything was going to be just dandy.

"But Mr. Goldwyn, we haven't talked money," Doc remarked.

"Don't worry about money," said Sam. "I'll give him anything he wants."

"Bob Hope wants a hundred thousand," Al Melnick announced.

Sam rose calmly, walked to the side of his office, and began hitting his head against the wall. When he finished with this exercise, he returned to his desk.

"Forget it," Sam said. "Our conversation is over."

Doc and Al persisted. Sam made counteroffers. Doc and Al got up to leave. Sam urged them to stay. After an hour of negotiations, the conference ended with an agreement to disagree.

As soon as Doc Shurr returned to his office, there was a call from Sam Goldwyn. "Louie, are you alone?" Sam asked.

"Yes, I'm alone," Doc replied.

"Louie, you and I are going to have trouble with Melnick," Sam said.

Sam didn't realize what trouble he was in. The showdown came in Texas, where I went to help him premiere a Gary Cooper movie, *The Westerner*. We did four shows in Fort Worth and four in Dallas. Just before the last show, I said to Sam, "I'd like to get an agreement on what you're going to pay me."

"Later, Bob, later," he said. I could tell he was in a good mood, so I devised a plan.

I gave him an introduction that made him sound like a combination of Thomas Edison, Flo Ziegfeld, and Albert Schweitzer. Sam came onstage glowing, and he told the huge audience, "I haven't made a comedy since I had Eddie Cantor—because I never found a comedian who could do as well. Now I have found one—Bob Hope."

That's when I got into his act. "That's very nice, Sam," I said, "but let's talk money."

"Not now, Bob," Sam said. "Later."

"Not later. Now. These folks won't mind. Come on, Sam, let's get a little more comfortable."

I grabbed the microphone and lay down on the stage floor. "Won't you join me, Sam?" I said.

Sam always liked to appear distinguished, but there was a bit of the pixy in him, too—that's where the Goldwynisms came from. The audience roared as Sam got down on the stage with me. We conversed about my salary, then I got up and announced, "Folks, it will be a great pleasure for me to make a picture for Mr. Goldwyn."

The audience was screaming, and a *Life* photographer came out and shot the bizarre sight. We went to a party afterward, and one of the guests from Hollywood was William R. Wilkerson, publisher of the *Hollywood Reporter*.

Wilkerson chastised Sam: "Sam, how could you, a leader of the motion picture community, allow yourself to take part in such a silly stunt? You ought to be ashamed of yourself."

51

The statesman won out over the pixy. Sam ordered the photographer to kill the pictures.

After making fifteen pictures at Paramount, it was a big change to move over to Sam Goldwyn's smaller lot for *They Got Me Covered*. But it wasn't such a shock, because I took along that old gang of mine—Dotty Lamour, Dave (BBB) Butler, and Barney Dean.

The change of studios had Barney worried, and he tried to stay out of the way of Sam Goldwyn. But on the first day of shooting, Sam spied Barney on the set and demanded, "What do you do?"

"I'm a writer, sir," Barney said shakily.

"Well, don't just sit there—write something!"

One of the first scenes in the picture was in a restaurant, and Dotty's line was: "I'll have a scotch and soda." The bon vivant as usual, I said, "And bring two straws."

After we rehearsed the scene, I noticed a visitor conferring with Dave Butler. When we got ready for a take, Dave told Dotty to order a bourbon and soda. It seemed strange to me, but I didn't think anything about it until the next day when a case of bourbon was delivered to my house. Others on the picture got the same treatment. An interesting lesson in the power of motion pictures.

One day while we were shooting *They Got Me Covered*, Danny Kaye dropped in for a visit. He was a sensational new comic who had just starred on Broadway in *Let's Face It*, which was going to be my next picture at Paramount. I noticed that Danny seemed disconsolate.

"I'm going back to New York," he said.

"Why?" I asked. "I heard you were getting a contract with Goldwyn."

"I was, but I just saw my test. I look like a stiff. I felt uneasy because they wouldn't let me move in front of the camera. That's not my style. I've got to have movement."

"Gee, I think you'd be great in pictures. Don't give up so easily. You ought to get Dave Butler to shoot a test with you. He's great with comedy."

I made a suggestion to Dave, and he was delighted to make a test with Danny at the end of shooting that day.

Danny brought his wife Sylvia to play the piano for one of his standard numbers. Dave had the scene lighted, and he said, "Okay, let's start."

"Where do you want me to stand?" Danny asked.

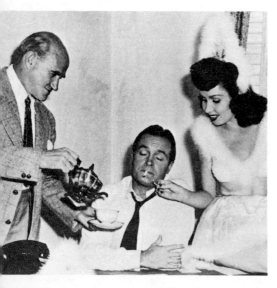

They Got Me Covered
(with Samuel Goldwyn
and Goldwyn Girl)

52

"Anywhere you want," Dave said. "I've got the camera on a
dolly, and you can stand or move as you wish. The camera will
follow *you*." Danny performed the number with his usual, free-
wheeling style, and the test was enough to convince Sam Goldwyn that he had a new star.

Let's Face It (with Eve Arden)

After *Let's Face It*, I returned to Samuel Goldwyn for a second
picture, *The Princess and the Pirate*.

It all started with an idea of Sy Bartlett's. He had heard a sup-

The Princess and the Pirate
(with Victor McLaglen)

posedly true story about a photographer assigned to shoot a famous novelist. The two got drunk together, and the novelist committed suicide by jumping out the window of his hotel. When the photographer woke up from his drunk, he found himself accused of murder. He cleared himself when police discovered the novelist had written his will on the photographer's chest in red pencil.

Sy switched the idea to having a pirate's map tattooed on my chest. He told the story to me, and I liked it. So we had a story conference with Sam and Niven Busch, his story editor.

Sy tells a good story, and he had Busch and me laughing our heads off. But Sam wasn't amused. Finally Sy came to a sequence which he admitted was a steal from an old sketch that Maurice Chevalier did with Mistinguett.

Busch and I were holding our sides with laughter, but Sam was giving Sy the Mount Rushmore treatment. "I don't think it's funny," Sam said.

"But Mr. Goldwyn, audiences have roared at this routine," Sy protested.

"Bartlett," Sam replied, "I have heard audiences roar with hate!"

Shortly afterward, Sy Bartlett enlisted in the Air Force. "Coward!" I told him. "What some guys will do to get away from Sam Goldwyn!"

The Princess and the Pirate was a lot of fun to do, especially because I got to appear in a lot of disguises. Of course, I had used many disguises in my vaudeville days, mainly for leaving town. This time I got paid for it.

I was really impressed with what a good disguise artist I was when Dolores visited the set with our children Linda and Tony. I was wearing the pirate's beard and costume as the Hook. Tony took one look, didn't recognize me, and broke out crying. And he hadn't even seen my rushes!

Sam Goldwyn was a lot of fun to work with. He even went along with a publicity gag about serving me tea every afternoon. That wasn't quite accurate. Sam was a taskmaster who made sure that his pictures were made with deliberate speed—and well. Only once did I get the better of him.

We were shooting two days of retakes on *The Princess and the Pirate*. Sidney Lanfield was directing, because Dave Butler had to make another assignment. After the first day's shooting, I said to Sidney: "You know what tomorrow is."

"No—what?" Sidney said.

"The USC-UCLA football game."

"But Bob, we've got a lot of scenes to shoot!"

"Give me the lines. I'll do it."

"But what about Goldwyn?"

"Don't worry. I'll handle Sam."

The next morning, Sam came on the set beaming. He had liked the previous day's shooting except for one shot he wanted redone.

"Okay, Sam, but we've got to finish by one o'clock," I said.

"Quit at one o'clock!" he said. "What for?"

"This afternoon is a holiday. Didn't you know that?"

"A holiday! For what?'

"The USC-UCLA football game."

The Princess and the Pirate
(with Linda, Tony, and Dolores Hope)

"For that they declare a holiday?"

"Sure thing, Sam. It's a quaint old California custom."

Sam went back to his office shaking his head. "Some holiday!" he said. Sidney finished the last retake at the stroke of one, and the entire crew took off for the Coliseum.

By 1945, my movie career was going like bagels at a B'nai B'rith picnic. With the radio show going great guns, too, I was earning $10,000 a week and well on my way to becoming the poorest millionaire in America. I was simply a way station between Paramount and Pepsodent on the one hand, and Uncle Sam on the other. In fact, the Internal Revenue Service stationed a man on the set to take control of my salary. Not that I minded financing all those battleships and bombers. I just wanted to hold onto the long green a little while longer before I handed it over.

Paramount didn't see it my way.

The boss of the studio, Y. Frank Freeman, used to come on the movie set and kneel down before me and ask, "Massa, what can Ah do foh you today?" I'd tap him on the shoulder with my putty knife and say, "Rise, slave."

All this was in a kidding vein, of course. Frank didn't know that I was planning a little surprise for him.

My attorney, Martin Gang, had figured out that the only way I could keep some of the money I was earning would be to form my own production company and make pictures in partnership with Paramount. That was unheard of in those days when the studios hired actors for straight salaries, refusing to cut anyone in on the profits. I suspected I would have a fight on my hands.

I invited Freeman to lunch at Perino's, the poshiest restaurant in Los Angeles. After he had taken a bite of his corn pone, I sprang my surprise on him.

"Frank, I'm going to form my own company and produce pictures," I said.

You'd think I had just called Jefferson Davis a horse thief.

"Now why would yo' want to do a thing lak thet?" he asked.

"For money," I replied. "So I can start saving some dough for myself and my family."

Freeman shook his head. "It ain't gonna work, Bob. We jest won't allow it. Now, I want to talk to yo' about this picture we want yo' to do—*Duffy's Tavern*—"

"Frank, you don't seem to get *my* picture. I want to make pictures for my own company."

"There's no way you can do that, Bob. If you insist, we'll have no choice but to suspend you."

"Too late. I'm suspending Paramount."

And I did. For a whole year, I didn't make a picture. There was no problem in keeping busy. I had the radio show, and I was traveling all over the world to do my thing for the GIs.

Finally, Freeman gave in. I formed Hope Enterprises, which would produce a certain number of pictures in partnership with Paramount. On other pictures I would work as a contract player. It was a great step forward for me, and not only financially. For the first time, I would have some voice in the preparation of my films. It was a good feeling.

In forming Hope Enterprises, I sold shares to various friends and associates, including Barney Dean. We even had meetings of the shareholders, usually in my dressing room at Paramount. At one of the meetings, Barney inquired: "When do we cut up the lemon?"

I think he meant to say melon, instead of lemon. But if you've seen some of my movies, you can't be sure.

What better way to return to the Paramount campus but with another *Road*. To *Utopia,* this time, with Hal Walker as our tour guide.

Now that I was no longer a mere employee, I had a slightly different attitude toward Paramount. Some days I became almost as nonchalant as Bing. Together, we were a deadly combination.

I came to the set one Friday morning and said to Bing, "You know who's playing tomorrow, don't you?"

"Sure," Bing said, "USC and Notre Dame."

"Well?"

That afternoon Bing said to the assistant director, "You know, my back has been killing me ever since Bob and I fell off that mountain. I think I'd better go see the doctor tomorrow. If I don't do something about it, I may be out all next week."

"Sure thing, Bing," the assistant said. "We'll schedule Dotty's song tomorrow."

On Saturday afternoon, Bing and I were sitting on the 50-yard line munching hot dogs. "How's your back, Bing?" I asked.

"Getting better all the time, Bob," he replied.

Our habits were a bit tough on Dotty Lamour. One day she was in makeup and costume to do a musical number with Bing and Bob. No Bing and Bob. We were off doing a benefit golf match.

57

The Road to Utopia
(with Dorothy Lamour
and Bing Crosby)

In midafternoon, Dotty was still waiting—and getting more and more furious. Gary Cooper ambled onto the set and asked what was going on. She told him.

"If I were you, I'd take a walk," Coop advised. "Go to your dressing room, take off your makeup and costume, and get the hell out."

Dotty did just that. She stormed out of the stage and was tramping down the street when she passed a visiting sailor. He didn't notice how mad she was, and he said, "Oh, Miss Lamour, I never expected to see you like this!"

"Neither did I!" she snapped. "That's what I get for working with those two idiots."

Bing and I sent her flowers to calm her down, and we promised to improve our work habits. And we did. For almost three days.

The Road to Utopia was written by the two gag writers I started in Hollywood, Norman Panama and Mel Frank. Two bright young guys. Also very sneaky. They came to me and told me the story idea, making it appear that I would be the leading character. Then they described the script to Bing in such a way that he had the biggest part. Then they did the same to Dotty. Needless to say, our acceptance was unanimous.

Panama and Frank wrote some wild stuff for *Utopia*—everything including a talking fish. Their wildest sequence was the ending. The way they wrote it, the villain ties Dotty to a log in a sawmill. Bing and I arrive to save her from the buzz saw, and we measure hands on an ax handle like a baseball bat, to see which one will make the rescue. Fade-out. Years later, Bing and I are walking in a garden with Dotty in the middle. We part, and Bing walks off with half of Dotty, I walk off with the other half.

"I think it's great!" said Buddy DeSylva, who was head of production. But a few weeks later, he said, "I've got the finish."

The idea was that a crack in the ice pack would separate Bing on one side and Dotty and me on the other. Years later, Dotty and I are long married when Bing pays us a visit. We introduce our son, who turns out to look exactly like Bing.

"But Buddy, you'll never get that past the censors!" I said.

"Just watch us," he said confidently. And he did.

For *Utopia*, Panama and Frank wrote the famous line of all the *Roads*. It happens when Bing and I are posing as a couple of killers in the Klondike. He tells me to act tough when we go into a bar.

"What'll you have?" asks the heavy, Douglas Dumbrille.

The Road to Utopia
(with Douglas Dumbrille
and Bing Crosby)

Publicity Photo

"Couple of fingers of rotgut," Bing mutters.

"I'll take a lemonade," I say, adding quickly, "in a dirty glass!"

Mel Frank tells me that line has haunted him. When he went to England to make films, he expected interviewers to be impressed that he had directed and produced films with Cary Grant, Danny Kaye, Bing Crosby, Bob Hope, etc. Instead, he was written up as "the man who wrote the line, 'I'll take a lemonade—in a dirty glass.'"

Bob Hope in a Rudolph Valentino role?

That's like casting Phyllis Diller as Camille. (Come to think of it, she *does* have a good cough.)

The idea of my doing *Monsieur Beaucaire* originated with Sol Siegel, who was a Paramount producer as well as a brave man. Sol put Norman Panama and Mel Frank on the script, then Paul Jones took over as producer.

Panama and Frank had handed in sixty pages of script when they were notified that another writer was also working on the picture. It was common in those days for studios to assign several writers to a project, but the Writers Guild required that the original scripters be notified. Panama and Frank blew their tops and said they wouldn't finish the script—even though they had written the final thirty pages. Now Paramount was stuck without an ending to *Monsieur Beaucaire*. The studio boss was now Henry Ginsberg (Paramount's executive suite had a revolving door in those years). He made peace with Panama and Frank, who submitted the final pages but insisted on their freedom. That was the start of their careers as producers and directors, as well as writers.

All this happened while I was in Europe. When I returned, I was presented with a script that was hilarious. But I was worried about undertaking a costume picture that had once starred Valentino.

Fortunately, I was in good hands—George Marshall's. George had just the right touch for this kind of nonsense. The first preview was good, but everyone thought the picture could be improved. Frank Tashlin, a onetime cartoonist who became a screen writer, was assigned to dream up some sight gags, especially for the dueling climax between Joseph Schildkraut and me. I thought the duel was going a bit far-out in the slapstick department, but it played beautifully at the next preview. This was the start of a long association with Frank Tashlin.

Monsieur Beaucaire (with Joseph Schildkraut)

Monsieur Beaucaire seemed to please everyone—except my friend Douglas Fairbanks, Jr.

"Dash it all, Bob, he complained, "I was planning to do *Beaucaire* myself—straight. After your version, I wouldn't dare."

Those who have followed my career realize that I am among the most publicity-shy of performers. I hate to see my name in print, and I do everything I can to avoid interviews. If there is to be any publicity surrounding my name, I want it to come naturally. At least that's what I tell my eight press agents.

Seriously, folks—press people and publicists are among my best friends. Always have been. I have two prize possessons. One is the Golden Apple, which was presented to me by the Hollywood Women's Press Club for being the most co-operative actor in Hollywood. I also have a pair of cuff links which are my good-luck charms. They bear the image of St. Genesius, the patron who looks after us acting folk (what a job that is!). They were presented to me by the guys and gals of the Paramount publicity department in appreciation of our mutually helpful relationship over the years.

From my earliest days in Hollywood I have enjoyed the friendship of the press. I got along fine with Louella Parsons, a great lady who made the entire world her sewing circle—without giving too much needle. Hedda Hopper was another pal; she went along on four or five of my Christmas tours and she was always great fun. I miss them both.

Over the years I've gone along on large numbers of stunts that publicists have dreamed up. One of the most successful was for the opening of *My Favorite Brunette*. For weeks on my radio show, we ran a contest for people to answer, "Why I would like the premiere of *My Favorite Brunette* in my living room."

Thousands of entries poured in. The winner was a dentist's wife

My Favorite Brunette
(with Peter Lorre)

in Bellaire, Ohio. She turned out to be the richest woman in town, and she had a living room that could handle a hundred people. It was a wild scene.

I went all-out for *My Favorite Brunette* because it was the first production of Hope Enterprises. I even went to the extreme of paying Bing Crosby $25,000 for a twenty-second scene. I wanted him to play the executioner who almost gives me the gas. Bing said he'd do it only if I'd cough up the cash for his alma mater, Gonzaga University. The scholastic highbinder.

Our fifth *Road* took us to Rio. You know why they were called *Road* pictures? Because Dotty Lamour was always giving us the Stop sign.

The Road to Rio was an entirely different ball game for Bing and me. This time his company and mine each owned one third of the picture, and Paramount owned the other third.

On the first four *Road* pictures, we sometimes gave the assistant directors fits. As soon as the director called "Cut! Lunch!" Bing and I split. I hustled across Melrose Avenue to Lucey's restaurant for lunch with my writers or business associates. Bing cut out for the driving range at the Wilshire Country Club, about a mile away.

After the one-hour lunch break, the director would say, "Round 'em up." Then the poor assistant director had to get on the phone and start cajoling Bing and me to come back to the stage. If I happened to be in the middle of a radio script or Bing was hitting his nine-iron really well, it could take time. The assistant directors started calling us fifteen minutes before we were really needed, but even that trick didn't work.

All that changed when we became one-third owners of *The Road to Rio*. Bing and I hardly left the set, except to go to the men's room. At precisely sixty minutes after lunch was called, Bing would say, "All right, let's get moving. What are we waiting for?"

I would chime in: "Let's start shooting. Come on, we're wasting time."

Bing and I were partners in other businesses as well. We had both invested in a Texas oil venture that had brought us money by the gusher. We found another promising investment, a soft drink called Lime Cola. A promoter from Montgomery, Alabama, convinced us to invest $25,000 apiece with the promise that he was going to put Coca-Cola out of business.

The Road to Rio
(enjoying Lime Cola
with Bing Crosby
and Bob Feller)

APALACHICOLA, FLA.

Lyrics by JOHNNY BURKE · music by JAMES VAN HEUSEN

Paramount Pictures present
BING DON DOROTHY
CROSBY · HOPE · LAMOUR
and the
ANDREWS SISTERS
"ROAD TO RIO"
A PARAMOUNT RELEASE

BURKE AND VAN HEUSEN, INC. *Music Publishers*
1619 BROADWAY, NEW YORK 19, N. Y.

The thought occurred to us: why not use *The Road to Rio* to help sell Lime Cola?

Why not indeed? We ordered a large sign to be displayed prominently in one of the scenes.

"You can't do that!" argued the Paramount attorney, Jack Karp. "That's advertising!"

"We can't do that, huh?" I said. "Say, Bing—who owns this picture?"

"Why, you own a third, and I own a third," Bing replied.

"Let's see—one third and one third makes two thirds, right? I guess Paramount is outvoted."

The Lime Cola ad remained in *The Road to Rio*. Unfortunately, Lime Cola didn't put Coca-Cola out of business: Lime Cola went out of business itself. Bing's and my 25 Gs were gone with the wind.

There was no way to remove the Lime Cola ad from the picture. When the sign came on the screen at the preview, the only thing Bing and I could do was slump down in our seats and crawl up the aisle on our hands and knees.

As with all the *Roads*, the *Rio* set was heavily populated with visitors. I never realized how many visitors we had until one day when we were doing a carnival scene. The stage was jammed with extras, and the crew was taking a long time to light the set. Bing and I could have played eighteen holes of golf in the time that they were taking. Finally, I said, "What's taking so long?"

"It's a big scene," Hal Walker said. "It takes time to light."

At last the gaffer—he's the guy who directs the electricians—announced that the scene was lighted. Hal Walker said on the loudspeaker, "All right, this will be a take. Will the visitors please step back?"

A small army retreated from the set. "My God," said the gaffer, "I lighted all those visitors. I thought they were extras!"

I laughed and laughed—until I realized that one third of the production cost was coming out of my pocket. Then I had a nice little cry.

The Paleface had a lot of things going for it. Among the most outstanding: Jane Russell, a Howard Hughes discovery. He was looking at the mountains one day and a couple of them moved. We also had a wild and wacky script by Edmund Hartmann and Frank Tashlin, the light-handed direction of Norman McLeod— and "Buttons and Bows."

I'm convinced that the song had a great deal to do with the immense success of *The Paleface*. "Buttons and Bows" was released before the picture. By the time *The Paleface* opened at the Paramount Theater in New York, "Buttons and Bows" had been the number-one song on the Hit Parade for several weeks. The song got as much billing as Jane and I did.

"Buttons and Bows" was written by Jay Livingston and Ray Evans, two contract song writers who must have felt as if they were working in Siberia. You can imagine their envy of Johnny Burke and Jimmy Van Heusen, who got to write songs for Paramount's big musical star, Bing Crosby. Livingston and Evans were assigned to pen tunes for the resident comedian, Hope.

But I must say that Jay and Ray didn't let it depress them. In fact, they were more than eager. The first of the twelve pictures of mine they worked on was *Monsieur Beaucaire*. They were supposed to report for work on a Monday. But they were so excited about going to work for Paramount that they wrote all three songs on the weekend before they started the contract.

The Paleface (with Jane Russell)

Variety Girl　One Sunday in 1947, Paramount gathered all its contract players for a circus scene in *Variety Girl*, a movie that showed the good works done by the Variety Clubs. How many can you recognize? Some hints: During that time, the Paramount contract list included such names as William Bendix, Howard Da Silva, Macdonald Carey, Barry Fitzgerald, Cecil Kellaway, Sterling Hayden, George Reeves, William Demarest, Billy

De Wolfe, Patric Knowles, John Lund, Mikhail Rasumny, Alan Ladd,
Veronica Lake, Mona Freeman, Stanley Clements, Dorothy Lamour, Gail
Russell, Sonny Tufts, William Holden, Joan Caulfield, Gary Cooper, Mary
Hatcher, Olga San Juan, Lizabeth Scott, Burt Lancaster, Frank Faylen . . .
as well as a couple of newcomers named Crosby and Hope.

SET VISITORS

William Holden (*The Lemon Drop Kid*)

Cary Grant (*That Certain Feeling*)

Clark Gable (*The Princess and the Pirate*)

Helen Hayes and James MacArthur (*My Favorite Spy*)

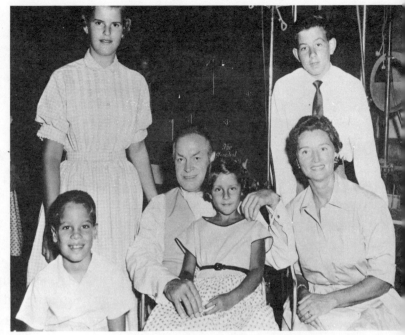

The Hope Clan (*The Seven Little Foys*)

The Crosby Boys (*The Road to Utopia*)

James Cagney and Danny Kaye (*The Seven Little Foys*)

Fred Astaire (*Fancy Pants*)

Buttons and Bows

Words and Music by JAY LIVINGSTON and RAY EVANS

SCORE
BUTTONS AND BOWS
MEETCHA 'ROUND THE CORNER

SPECIAL PICTURE RELEASE

From the Paramount Picture
BOB HOPE and JANE RUSSELL
in "THE PALEFACE"
In Technicolor

FAMOUS MUSIC CORP., • 1619 BROADWAY, New York City, N. Y.

For *The Paleface*, I needed a song to sing to Jane Russell while I was driving a wagon and she was in back. It could have been any song, as long as it was in keeping with the period.

Jay and Ray consulted a dictionary of Indian terms and came up with the expression "Everything's gonna be snookum," meaning it will all turn out fine. They whipped up a western rhythm song on that theme and played it for Norman McLeod, our producer, Robert Welch, and me.

"No good," Norman said. "We can't have Bob sing a comedy Indian song and then have the Indians play the menace in the next reel."

"Look, fellas," said Bob Welch, who was a big, bubbling man full of fun. "Why don't you write a song that has a lot of bounce, like that one from *Oklahoma!*—'Kansas City'? Maybe something that will carry out the theme that Bob is a city boy out West and he yearns for the East, where women wear pretty clothes."

Back to the drawing board for Livingston and Evans. As they returned to their office in the music building, Ray suggested a title: "Buttons and Bows." They sat down in their office and completed the phrase: "Frills and flowers and buttons and bows, rings and things and buttons and bows." Then Jay started to write a musical phrase to lead into it.

Three weeks later, he was still trying. Jay tells me that it's hard to write the last half of a song first and then try to find music to lead into it. Finally the boys came up with the phrase "East is east and west is west," and that led Jay into the melody.

As soon as I heard, "Buttons and Bows," I said, "This is it, boys." Jay taught me the tune, I recorded it, and we shot the number for the picture.

In those years, Paramount had a big backlog of pictures, and *The Paleface* wasn't released for more than a year. Meanwhile Livingston and Evans were sitting on "Buttons and Bows," wondering how to make it a hit.

The boys decided they wanted Dinah Shore to make a record of the song. They played it for her, and she liked it. But there was a problem: a musicans' strike was going to shut down all recording. Dinah recorded "Buttons and Bows" with eight musicians improvising a background. She finished a couple of minutes before the midnight deadline that started the strike.

Dinah's record was a big smash, and there I was without a recording of my own hit song! I finally made a record for Capitol, singing all by myself in the lounge of the Capitol building. I used earphones to listen to the music, which had been recorded in Mexico.

"Buttons and Bows" went on to win the Oscar for the best movie song of 1948, and it has been following me ever since. Livingston and Evans wrote parody lyrics which I still use in personal appearances.

I became aware of the international impact of "Buttons and Bows" when I went to Japan in 1951. As I was driving from the airport to Tokyo, Japanese boys pedaled alongside on bicycles and sang "Buttons and Bows" to me. It sounded very strange, because the Japanese had translated the lyrics except for the title phrase.

The real thrill came in Osaka, when I played to thousands of people at a huge swimming-pool stadium. One side was filled with American GIs and the other side was jammed with Japanese civilians. When I sang the song, several thousand Japanese joined me in singing the only American words of the song they knew— the title phrase.

Our director on *The Paleface*, Norman McLeod, was the most un-director-like of directors. Compared to Norman, Don Knotts would seem like Don Rickles. But for all his quiet manner, Norman was a brilliant director of comedy, and a great guy to work with.

I liked to tease Norman by calling him "Noisy." I remember especially a day when we were doing a rough scene in which a team of horses was supposed to drag me off a wagon. We were doing it on a huge indoor stage—actually two stages back to back.

Nothing worked. The trick equipment for staging the stunt fell apart, the horses wouldn't behave, and the arc lamps sputtered and ruined the takes. It was late Friday afternoon after a hard week's work, and in those days you could call it quits at 5 P.M. if you were a star.

I said to Jane Russell: "How do you feel?"

"I'm a little tired," she admitted.

"Okay, that's all for today," I announced.

The assistant director froze. Norman McLeod seemed stunned.

"See you tomorrow, Noisy," I said, and I began walking to the door at the other end of the stage. It was a long walk, down the dusty western street.

Norman kept staring at me. Finally, as I reached the door a

71

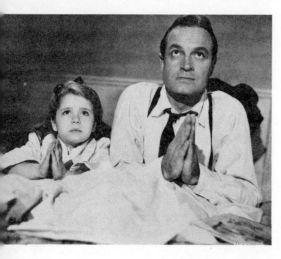

Sorrowful Jones
(with Mary Jane Saunders)

hundred yards away, he stamped his foot and said in his semi-whisper, "Bob, you come back here!"

The crew told me about it the next day—the ones who were close enough to hear him.

Sorrowful Jones was memorable for two reasons: it was my first time out in a semi-serious role; and it was my first movie with Lucille Ball.

The story was from Damon Runyon, and I had a great fondness for him. I got to know him when we lived at the same hotel in New York, back in the early 1930s. And his rave for "Thanks for the Memory" in *The Big Broadcast of 1938* had saved my movie career.

Sorrowful Jones was based on the Shirley Temple picture *Little Miss Marker*. The script called for me to play a hard-bitten bookie who gets stuck with playing baby-sitter for a little girl. One of the toughest scenes I had to do was a prayer with the girl, who was a young charmer named Mary Jane Saunders. Sidney Lanfield, who was directing, insisted that I play it straight—no gags this time. I guess it impressed my fellow workers at Paramount, because the word got around that I had been taking lessons at the Mickey Rooney Academy of Dramatic Arts. That wasn't true. I had plenty of experience playing dramatic scenes in booking offices all over the country.

I was delighted to find myself working with Lucille Ball. We had appeared together at a camp show during the war, but *Sorrowful Jones* was really the first time we became acquainted. I had known her husband, Desi Arnaz, because he and his band were regulars on my radio show for a while. During that time I kept telling my writers, "Give Desi some lines on the show." They kept telling me, "The guy can't read lines; he'd bomb." Not long after that, Desi demonstrated his ability to handle lines on a show called "I Love Lucy."

Another delight in *Sorrowful Jones* was William Demarest. What a character! He and I used to swap vaudeville stories. One of my favorites was one he told about the time he was playing Winnipeg, Canada, and he preceded an act called "Lady Alice's Cockatoos and Macaws." These birds were trained to answer questions that Lady Alice put to them. The trouble was that they had to be set up on their perches behind the curtain while Bill Demarest was doing his comedy act out in front. And, not being acquainted with the deportment of the theaters, they chattered among themselves while waiting for their performance.

Nothing bothers a comedian so much as extraneous noise while he's trying to do his act. The bird noises bugged Bill so much that he muttered, "Keep those birds quiet back there!" The birds kept chattering, and Bill's act died.

Bill tried everything to get rid of the noisy birds; he even wired the booking office in New York to try to break his contract. No luck. But he got his revenge. One night before the performance, he had a private coaching system with the birds. And when Lady Alice asked her questions before the audience that night, the answers she got were "—— you!"

Comedians everywhere

"Bob, your next picture is going to be a fantasy," the producer told me.

"Oh, that sounds interesting," I said. "What's it called?"

"The Great Lover."

I told him *I* was supposed to be the comedian. I felt a little better when he told me Rhonda Fleming was going to be my leading lady. Rhonda was making a comeback—she had just done a picture with Bing Crosby. She was surprised that we did our love scenes so fast. They didn't have to stop to give *me* adrenalin shots.

Rhonda was a sweet girl, but I think she had *The Great Lover* mixed up with my previous picture. Whenever I asked her how I was doing in the love scenes, she said, "Sorrowful."

The Great Lover

Working with Lucille Ball is always fun and games. But on *Fancy Pants*, the games turned out to be no fun.

I should have known what I was in for when George Marshall directed a scene in which I was surrounded by Indians. George himself threw the hatchets and arrows at me. He came so close, I thought my ski nose was going to be turned into a sled. If there had been an Oscar for sheer terror that year, nobody could have beaten me.

One of my feet got stepped on by a horse, the other by Bruce Cabot, who was built like one. Eight years later, I underwent operations to repair both feet.

The worst came not from a real horse, but a wooden one.

Lucille was supposed to be teaching me to ride on a barrel. The thing was 7 feet off the floor, and George Marshall wanted it to go faster and faster, for realism's sake. You've heard of runaway horses. This mechanical beast got its AC and DC mixed up and

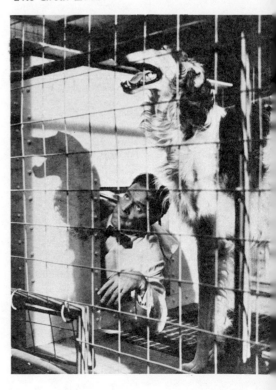

started galloping like a two-year-old in heat. The next thing I knew, I was spread-eagled on the cement floor.

An ambulance rushed me to Hollywood Presbyterian Hospital, where X rays found nothing broken but my morale. As I was resting up from the aches and pains, I used the time to compose a letter to Henry Ginsberg, latest in the Long Gray Line of Paramount production chiefs:

Dear Henry,

First I want to thank you for your kindness during my recent illness and tell you that you did not have to do it, I wasn't going to sue in the first place. For a while, I was a little bitter, I will admit, realizing that if your production heads had used a real horse instead of a broken-down barrel I would not have ended on my back on Stage 17 with an injury which you will see from the bill I am enclosing was not cheap . . .

Inasmuch as you are going to have to explain my $4,500 doctors' bills at the next stockholders meeting—assuming you are still with the company—I think I should explain that they are not out of line.

Now you and I know that in the old days when a man fell on his back he merely got up, tightened his belt, and walked back into the bar. Alas, that is the old way. Let me reveal to you the great stride medicine has made during our generation.

When I woke up in the hospital, four nurses were standing over me, a doctor was feeling my pulse, while another doctor—a specialist, I learned—was busy on the phone checking with the Bank of America on how much we would go for . . .

Now they started the procession of tests which you will find on page 3 of the bill. Originally I just had a pain in my back, but as they kept monkeying around with me, the pain kept getting lower and lower. Meantime, no one would tell me how I was doing. I finally picked up the phone, got an outside wire, called the hospital and asked how Bob Hope was doing. It didn't help any to find out that I'd taken a turn for the worse.

The X rays were a little confusing at first. My chest kept showing up the figure 24.2. I had forgotten to tell them that I'd had the rating of last year's radio show tattooed over my heart. The more X rays they took, the more the doctor looked worried. It seems they couldn't find anything wrong with me, and he'd promised his wife a new mink coat.

He finally got desperate one day. When he thought I was dozing, I heard him scream at the X-ray technician, "Find something—even if it's in another patient!"

The whole staff was getting a little desperate when a little man who I later learned was a renegade from the Menninger Clinic finally decided I might be having a psychosomatic symptom. That's a new type of medicine they've just hit upon, Henry. That's when you don't have anything wrong with you but you think you have, and you think about it so hard it gets worse than if you really had it.

Confusing, isn't it? We've sure come a long way from sulphur and molasses, haven't we?

But I could see that I had them over a barrel at this point—if the word is not too sensitive to you—and with one longing look at my gall bladder, the doctors allowed me to go home.

The remainder of the bill will be self-explanatory, although I imagine the occupational therapy—$1,400—may be a little out of line. You see, Henry, the occupation that I picked up was horseplaying, and we both know that is not a poor man's pastime. Please understand that this puts me in deep debt to you, almost as deep as you are to the doctors.

Yours in our great work,
Bob Hope

Fancy Pants
(with Lucille Ball,
before the fall)

During those postwar years, leading film theaters in most of the major cities were still playing stage shows. So when I wasn't busy making pictures, doing my radio show, or touring army camps, I went back to playing theaters. That's where it all started for me, and I enjoyed returning to the scene of the crime.

The New York Paramount Theater was a particular favorite of mine. The manager for many years was Robert Weitman, now a successful movie producer. Bob and I became very good friends —and co-conspirators.

We liked to break records. Each booking at the New York Paramount was a challenge to see if we could draw more customers than the time before. When Bob Weitman came to my dressing room, I'd ask him, "How're we doing?"

"Take a look," he'd say, pointing out the window to the lines of people that went around the building. We could tell by the length of the lines exactly how good business was.

Bob's big problem were the "sit-overs." Those were the people who stayed in their seats during two stage shows, thus cutting down on the turnover. Bob had ways of combating that.

After the stage show ended, Don Baker played the mighty organ for a "follow the bouncing ball" community sing. He always finished with "The Star-Spangled Banner." That got people on their feet and inclined to move out.

Another trick was to announce that I would be handing out photographs outside my dressing room.

I remember one engagement at the New York Paramount when the crowds were enormous. But Bob Weitman and I were greedy. We wanted more.

SILVER BELLS

WORDS AND MUSIC BY JAY LIVINGSTON AND RAY EVANS

SCORE
Silver Bells
They Obviously Want Me To Sing
It Doesn't Cost A Dime To Dream

SPECIAL PICTURE RELEASE

From the Paramount Picture
"THE LEMON DROP KID"
starring Bob Hope and Marilyn Maxwell
Based on a story by Damon Runyon

PARAMOUNT MUSIC CORPORATION · 1619 Broadway · New York 19, N. Y.

"If we could squeeze in one more stage show, we could set a new record," I said.

"I'll see what I can do," said Bob.

The movie on the bill was a sea epic that ran 98 minutes. Bob went up to the projection booth and cut 12 minutes of waves out of the picture. The movie was running six times a day; that meant 72 added minutes, enough for another stage show. I was already doing six—seven on Saturday.

Bob Weitman had only one worry. During each engagement, all of the Paramount brass, including the president Barney Balaban and chairman-founder Adolph Zukor, came down in a special elevator from the Paramount offices and watched the show. Bob feared they would raise cain if they found out the picture had been cut.

The bosses came to see the show, and they congratulated Bob on the big crowds. Just before he went back into the elevator, little old Adolph Zukor said to Bob in a whisper, "You cut the picture, didn't you?"

"Yes, Mr. Zukor," Bob admitted.

Mr. Zukor smiled as he mentally counted the house. "It's good for business," he said.

The Lemon Drop Kid took me back to the Damon Runyon country that had proved successful with *Sorrowful Jones*. Once again Bob Welch produced and Sidney Lanfield directed. This time the leading lady was Marilyn Maxwell. What a doll she was. The kind of girl you could take home to your mother—after you locked your father in the garage.

All of the Paramount brass came to Hollywood for the preview of *The Lemon Drop Kid*. It was at the Westwood Village Theater and I remember standing out in front with Barney Balaban, the president of Paramount. "It's great, Bob," he said. "We can ship it to New York as is."

"Now wait a minute, Barney," I said. "Let's talk it over first." We went to the Beverly Hills Hotel for a drink, and I argued that the picture could profit from some additions. I must have argued pretty well, because Paramount went back for retakes that cost $200,000.

Frank Tashlin, whose wacky humor I admired, was assigned to do a rewrite. He ran the picture, together with a recording of the laughs from the preview. Then he put blank film in the picture where he planned the additions. Frank showed me *The Lemon*

Drop Kid that way, explaining what would be added to the blank scenes.

"Sounds good," I said. Bob Welch agreed.

"I'll do the rewrite," Frank said, "if you let me direct it."

We agreed, and that's how Frank Tashlin became a director.

One of the important things that Frank did to *The Lemon Drop Kid* was to restage the "Silver Bells" number. Jay Livingston and Ray Evans had been assigned to write a Christmas song, and they fought against it.

"The only way we can stay under contract to Paramount is to turn out hits," they argued. "How can we write a Christmas hit when Irving Berlin has the market sewed up with 'White Christmas'?"

But the Christmas sequence was necessary to the plot, and so they went to work. Looking for a different approach, they wrote the song in ¾ time instead of ¼, which was the time of most big Christmas songs. Instead of sleigh bells and yule logs, they made the lyrics about Christmas in the city. At first they called it "Tinkle Bell." But that sounded lousy. On their desk was a silver bell they had been given on a publicity junket. Eureka!

The Lemon Drop Kid

When we first shot the "Silver Bells" number, Marilyn and I sang it in the gambling casino with the rest of the cast on risers like a glee club. Tashlin brought in Nick Castle to choreograph the number on Paramount's New York street with falling snow, extras, and the whole works.

"Silver Bells" became a big hit. Just my luck—Bing Crosby made the first recording and took most of the play. Livingston and Evans tell me that the song has sold 31,800,000 records and 1,643,687 copies of sheet music.

The song they didn't want to write turned out to be their biggest seller.

In *My Favorite Spy* I played two parts, and both of them were Hedy Lamarr's lovers. How about that for overtime!

Son of Paleface (with Trigger)

Son of Paleface was the first time that Frank Tashlin directed a full-length picture. He was a very persuasive guy. For one scene, he wanted me to get in bed with Trigger.

"Oh no you don't!" I protested. "Bing and I got in bed with a bear on *The Road to Utopia,* and the beast nearly killed his trainer the next day."

"Bob," Frank said, "this is no ordinary horse. This is Trigger."

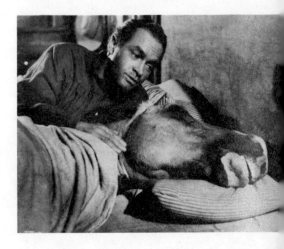

My Favorite Spy
(with Hedy Lamarr
and Francis L. Sullivan)

"I don't care if he's got an IQ of 150," I said. "He's liable to roll over and I'll be Pancake No. 5."

"Look—I'll show you how easy it is."

Frank climbed into the bed and snuggled up to Trigger. I watched him for a minute and said, "Okay. But if you don't get it in one take—that's all, brother."

Bing, Dotty, and I hadn't made a picture together in five years when Paramount decided to put us on *The Road to Bali*.

Bali was our first *Road* in color. Now the audience could see Bing's natural complexion—a rich shade of legal-tender green. He had a peculiar allergy that caused him to break out in annuities.

Once again Bing and I agreed to take Paramount in as a partner, and each of us owned one third of *The Road to Bali*. That could sometimes cause a dilemma, as when Bing and I went East one weekend for a telethon to benefit our Olympic Games team.

Son of Paleface
(with Roy Rogers
and Jane Russell)

The producer, Harry Tugend, came to us on Friday and said, "I suppose you boys won't be back for work on Monday."

"We'll try," Bing said.

"I've got to have a more definite answer," Harry insisted.

"Let's see, Har," I said; "if we don't show up Monday, one third of the money that's lost is Bing's, and one third is mine. Right?"

"Right," Harry said.

"We'll be here," I said.

P.S. We didn't make it.

Off Limits was a boxing picture, so I felt right at home. I was a boxer myself, you know. People ask me how I got my fighting name, Packy East. That was because when I finished a fight, my body was facing west and my head was facing east.

Mickey Rooney played the fighter in *Off Limits*. I found out why he was so short. His parents were in vaudeville, and Mickey was born in a trunk. But they lost the key.

The Road to Bali
(with Bing Crosby
and Dorothy Lamour)

Paramount had some doubts about hiring Mickey for the role. He had a reputation for liking the nightclub life, and the studio was worried that he might not prove reliable.

Harry Tugend, the producer of *Off Limits*, told me, "Mickey would be great for the part of the boxer—if he'll behave. I'm willing to take the gamble if you are."

"Absolutely," I said. "Mickey is one of the most talented actors in town."

"Okay, I'll go to bat for him with the front office," Harry said.

As I expected, Mickey was totally professional throughout the shooting. He faltered only one day. That was when we were shooting the Madison Square Garden fight with Jack Dempsey as referee and five hundred extras for the crowd. Mickey pulled a no-show.

The day's shooting was costing $10,000, and without Mickey it would have been wasted. Harry Tugend rushed to Mickey's apartment and found him sound asleep.

"I can't make it," Mickey croaked. "Got laryngitis."

"Okay, Mickey," said the producer, "but we've got to make sure it's laryngitis so Paramount can collect the insurance for the lost day. I'll call the studio doctor."

Mickey made a dramatic recovery. He boxed all day and fought like a tiger.

When *Off Limits* was released, the critics raved about the combination of Hope and Rooney. In fact, one reviewer in Washington said: "After all these years in movies, Hope *deserves* a Mickey."

I went back to swashbuckling with *Casanova's Big Night*, but I had a little trouble with the role. Every time I had to swash, I buckled.

Paramount was very worried about *Casanova's Big Night*. I had recently signed with NBC for a series of television specials, and some of the people in the movie industry treated me as if I was Tokyo Rose. I received poison pen letters from theater owners who said, "How could you sell out to the enemy?" At that time exhibitors were convinced that television could kill the movie business, just as movies had killed vaudeville.

Paramount decided to punish me, and the location of my dressing room was changed. I was really upset about it until I counted up my tips.

I told the bosses that it was a mistake to fight television, that

Off Limits (with Mickey Rooney)

Casanova's Big Night
(comparing profiles
with John Carradine
and Basil Rathbone)

the movie business should join hands with the new medium. They showed me the definition of "medium" in the dictionary: "A go-between that brings back the dead."

Barney Balaban, the president of Paramount, told me that *Casanova's Big Night* would lose a million dollars because the theater owners were sore at me for going on television. I guess they couldn't have been too terribly sore, because the picture earned more than $3 million.

Mel Shavelson and Jack Rose, who had written for my radio show and later wrote several films for me, came to me one day with the idea of my playing Eddie Foy. He was a vaudevillian who had put his seven children to work in his act—sort of a gaslight Bing Crosby.

The way Mel and Jack described it, the story would be pretty dramatic. Imagine W. C. Fields with seven kids, and you get a picture of Eddie Foy. After his Italian wife died, Foy was faced with the job of bringing up the children by himself. He solved the problem by starting the most famous family act in vaudeville.

"I like it," I told Mel and Jack.

"Then you're in trouble," Mel said.

"Why is that?"

"Because I want to break in as a director," Mel said.

"I'm willing to take a chance," I said.

"Then you're in more trouble," Jack said.

"Why is that?" I asked.

"Because you won't get any salary for the picture," Jack explained. "The way it's set up, we all get a percentage of the profits —if any."

I was willing to go along on the gamble, and so we sold the package to Paramount. I saw *The Seven Little Foys* as a real challenge. It was the first time I would play a real-life character, and I had some pretty heavy dramatics to perform. I wanted to capture Eddie Foy as well as I could, and I studied everything I could find about his life, including some silent movies he had made. I received a great deal of help from the Foys themselves, especially Bryan, Eddie Jr., and Charley, who was the technical adviser on the picture.

The toughest scene for me to do was when I had to plead with a judge for custody of my children, who had been taken from me because of child labor laws. It was a long, dramatic speech, quite a change of pace for a guy who was accustomed to one-liners. On

The Seven Little Foys

the night before I had to do the scene, Barney Dean died. I got through it.

When they were planning *The Seven Little Foys*, Shavelson and Rose got the bright idea of asking James Cagney to make a guest appearance as George M. Cohan. But how to approach him? Mel and Jack arranged a meeting and put the question to Jimmy.

"Sure, I'll do it," Jimmy replied. Mel and Jack were overjoyed until Jimmy added, "I'll do it on one condition."

"What's that?" Jack asked, fearing the worst.

"That I don't get paid," Jimmy said.

Mel and Jack couldn't believe their ears. "But why?" they asked.

"Because when I was breaking in as an actor," said Jimmy, "I could always get a square meal and a place to flop at the Foys'. This is my way of paying them back."

Mel was hesitant about the next question: "Would you do a dance number with Bob?"

84

Jimmy gave his wide Irish smile. "I just happen to have my tap shoes in my car. Where's the rehearsal hall?"

As I was making *The Seven Little Foys,* I used to poke my head in the rehearsal hall to see Jimmy rehearse. He was going at it as if it meant another Academy Award. If he was going to work so hard, I had to do the same. I never worked so hard for a dance number since my kid days in Cleveland.

The Seven Little Foys was worth all the labor. Not only did it place me in another category as a performer. It also made a mint of money—and Hope Enterprises owned 44 per cent of the take.

In 1955, I made *The Iron Petticoat* for M-G-M. What a shock to find out that Paramount wasn't my real mother!

This was my first picture outside the United States, and it was a real thrill to be making it in my native land, England. When I arrived at the London airport, I was greeted by the Bob Hope Fan Club. He turned out to be an awfully nice chap. All my English relatives were there to meet me, too, and the sight made me homesick for California—all those outstretched palms.

They took me to see the exact place where I was born, and it turned out to be a bomb crater. The thing that upset me most was that it had been bombed *before* the war. A fellow with a monocle walked by and said, "I say—are you Bob Hope?"

"That's right," I said, "England's gift to the United States."

"Good," he said, "that makes us even for the Boston Tea Party."

The Iron Butterfly had been written by Ben Hecht with Cary Grant in mind for the leading man. Cary wasn't available, so my name was suggested. "It's great casting!" Ben remarked after his wrists had been bandaged.

Katharine Hepburn had been signed for the role of the Russian pilot. I had never worked with her before, but I had heard a lot about her from Spencer Tracy. He was not a close friend of mine, but I felt that I knew him well because he was so cordial every time we met.

It was quite a thrill for me to be playing opposite such a distinguished actress as Katharine Hepburn. I was really nervous about appearing with such a big-leaguer, but she was very patient with me. She just sat there, polishing her Oscar.

Now she's got three of them. Unfair!

We had script problems on *The Iron Petticoat.* When I arrived in England, I telephoned Ben Hecht at his diggings in the Connaught Hotel and told him, "Ben, this script isn't finished."

The Seven Little Foys
(with James Cagney)

85

"I know," he replied, "but it's coming along."

I volunteered that I had some thoughts on how we could help the script. Within ten minutes, Ben barged into my suite at the Dorchester Hotel, accompanied by Katie Hepburn, his secretary, and a couple of assistants.

"Yes? Yes?" Ben said expectantly.

"Wait a minute!" I said. "It's not that large. I just had a couple of hokey thoughts about the script." It was then I realized what trouble we were in.

But we managed to get through the picture, and I must say that Katie was a gem. She played the Jewish mother on the set, fussing over anybody who happened to sneeze. I felt so ashamed at being so deucedly healthy that I felt like trying to get the grippe.

Paramount was in doubt whether I could play Jimmy Walker, the mayor of New York, in *Beau James*.

"Maybe Hope could play Eddie Foy—he was a vaudevillian," said one of the executives. "But Jimmy Walker was light, gay, carefree, full of charm and magnetism!"

Paramount considered several other actors before I got the part. It was the longest stockholders meeting we ever held.

I always wanted to produce a picture with a message, and I got my way with *Paris Holiday*. The message was: "Stick to acting."

The idea for the picture came to me when I myself was on a Paris holiday. I was visiting my old friend Maurice Chevalier, who said, "Boob"—you know how strangely he pronounced English—"I have someone who is your greatest fan and wants to meet you. His name is Fernandel, and he is the funniest man in all of France—until you arrived, of course."

I went to see Fernandel at his apartment, and he was indeed a fan. "I will do anything with you, Monsieur Opie," he said through an interpreter.

That started me thinking about a plot in which an American entertainer and a Frenchman become involved with beautiful girls and a spy ring. Ed Beloin and Dean Riesner wrote the script, and I produced.

This was my first experience in film financing, and I thought about calling the picture *Around the Bank of America in 80 Days*. But the bank wasn't too tough about terms. I only had to make three more pictures to get my children back.

When I went to Paris to start production, I presented the script to Fernandel. He couldn't read the English dialogue, but he counted up how many lines he had compared to mine.

"I must have more money," he announced. He was already getting $100,000, but he wanted $20,000 more—in cash.

How to find $20,000 in cash in Europe presented a problem. My agent, Louie Shurr, volunteered to go to Switzerland for the lettuce harvest. He took along Monte Brice, who had succeeded Barney Dean as gag man on my movies.

Shurr and Brice—what a pair! That was like sending Laurel and Hardy on a mission for the CIA.

Doc Shurr as an undercover agent was a panic. He bought himself a trench coat and had the $20,000 around his waist in a money belt. If he had fallen off his elevated shoes, he would have rolled all the way down the Alps.

The Doctor wouldn't let anyone get close to him. He wouldn't even ask the train station attendants for directions to the men's room. He and Monte made it back safely with the loot, and Fernandel's smile became even wider.

He and I got along just fine. Each morning we would greet each other on the set.

"Good morning, Bob," he said.

"Bonjour, Fernandel," I said.

That was it. Neither of us knew how to say anything else in the other's language. Yet we understood each other perfectly. There must be some kind of international language among comedians.

Paris Holiday set a new record: three men were killed on the picture. All of them auditors. The cost went a million dollars over budget, but it was United Artists' own fault. Handing me the money to make a movie is like asking Dean Martin to tend your bar.

I managed to do a better job of producing my next picture, *Alias Jesse James*. It came in under budget. *Alias Jesse James* was made at a time when adult Westerns were the rage of television. I had my own answer: I used older horses.

The Facts of Life was a daring picture for me. It was the story of two handicapped people who fall in love. Their handicaps were his wife and her husband.

Norman Panama and Mel Frank wrote the script—but not for Lucille Ball and me, the fools. Norman and Mel wanted to explore the adultery theme of *Brief Encounter* with an American story

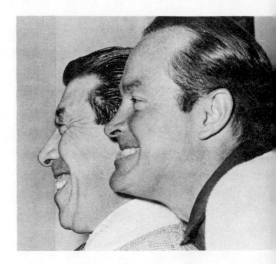

Paris Holiday (with Fernandel)

Alias Jesse James (with Rhonda Fleming)

that would star Olivia De Havilland and William Holden. The first two thirds was straight and the final third was to be funny.

"It might work if you can get the comedy out of the last third," Norman and Mel were told. But they couldn't seem to lick the problem. Then *Strangers When We Meet* came out with Kirk Douglas and Kim Novak in an adultery theme, so the two authors figured they had blown it.

Then Mel Frank woke up in the middle of the night and exclaimed: "I know how to save *The Facts of Life!*"

"How?" said his wife (she's part Indian).

"By making it with Bob Hope!"

"Great, Mel. Go back to sleep."

In the morning, Mel called his partner, who agreed it was a good idea. Then Mel called me. He has a voice that sounds exactly like mine on the telephone, so I sounded as if I were talking to myself.

"Hi," he said.

"What's up?" I said.

"Wanta hear a story?"

"How soon can you be here?"

"Twenty minutes."

"See ya."

Twenty minutes later, Mel and Norm were at my house telling me the story of *The Facts of Life.*

"It's a little straight, isn't it?" I said.

"Bob, that's the way it's funny," Norm insisted. "If you *try* to be funny, it won't work."

"Who do you have in mind for the woman?" I asked.

"Lucille Ball."

"If you can get her, I'll do it."

Panama and Frank went to Lucille that night and told her the story. She was crying when they finished.

"It's beautiful," she said. "Who do you having in mind for the man?"

"Bobe Hope."

"If you can get him, I'll do it. But there's just one thing."

"What's that?"

"I don't want it to be *The Road to Infidelity.*"

The deal was made. Half of the profits went to a very worthy cause—and Lucille got the other half. It was a lot different from when Lucille and I made *Sorrowful Jones* and *Fancy Pants* together. Now she was the biggest star in television, and she owned her own studio. It was the first time I had ever kissed a studio head—face to face.

We shot *The Facts of Life* at Desilu Studios. Both Lucy and I were determined to submerge our own personalities in the roles we were playing. After a scene, Lucille would ask Mel Frank, the director: "Was I 'Lucy'? Was I 'Lucy'?" She was anxious not to play the same role that had proved so popular on television.

About two weeks before the end of shooting, I remarked to Mel Frank, "You know something—this has been the smoothest picture I've ever worked on."

"Amazing, isn't it?" he said. "Everything has just gone bang-bang."

At that moment we heard a bang. Lucy was rehearsing a scene in which she was supposed to step into a rowboat. She fell 8½ feet, hit her head on the boat, and was knocked unconscious. She had black eyes, a bruised face, and a gashed leg.

The Facts of Life
(with Lucille Ball)

Bachelor in Paradise
(with Lana Turner
and Jim Hutton)

Filming had to be suspended for a month while Lucy recovered. During that time I caught my finger in a door, and Mel Frank sprained his ankle on the golf course. When we went back to work, Lucy needed heavy makeup to hide her injuries, I had my hand in a bandage, and Mel was on crutches. We looked like the original cast of *War and Peace*.

But *The Facts of Life* was worth all the injuries. It proved to be a big success, especially in drive-in theaters. Some of the cars were even turned toward the screen.

It was fun making *Bachelor in Paradise* with Lana Turner—she was between weddings at the time. The picture had its premiere in England, and it was also showing on the plane coming back. It was the first time I had seen one of my pictures on an airplane. I was surprised when the stewardess announced that *Bachelor in Paradise* was about to begin—then she handed out programs and containers.

At least nobody walked out.

It had been a long time between *Roads*—almost ten years. Then Norman Panama and Mel Frank came up with the idea for *The Road to Hong Kong*. The picture had everything—double-crossing, intrigue, drama, pathos, heartbreak. And that was just in getting the financing.

The picture was going to be made in England, and I decided to take my whole gang along: Dolores, Tony, Linda, Kelly, and Norah. That meant a housing problem, and I asked Mel Frank to find me a place to live. He located an old manor house called Cranbourne Court, which was decorated in early Wuthering Heights. Dolores saw the place first, and she fell in love with it. So did I, when I found out it was located in the middle of three golf courses.

When she first looked at Cranbourne Court, she came to the golf club where Bing and I had been playing. "I found the most divine house, and it's not far from here," she said.

"I'd like to look at it with you," said Bing. When he saw the place, he said, "Why don't we both move in?" And so Bing, Kathryn, and their youngsters joined the Hope brigade in an exercise in communal living.

We had a ball. In the morning, Bing and I sailed off to the studio, only fourteen minutes away, in our chauffeured Roll-Royce. Our wives and kiddies explored merry olde England while we toiled under the arc lamps. Well, it wasn't too terribly strenuous. When the English crew broke for tea in the afternoon, Bing and I took a golf break. We could usually get in nine holes before darkness fell over the bogs.

Then both families gathered in the dining room, which was big enough to hold a Roller Derby in. Cranbourne Court came fully equipped with china, silver, and full staff, including an Arthur Treacher-like butler who leaned toward the port. Every night the ham was glazed and so was the butler.

One day when I was playing golf at the Wentworth course, a messenger came out to the fifteenth tee to tell me that Zsa Zsa Gabor was waiting for me in the clubhouse. When I arrived, she said, "Bob, dahlink, I understand there is the most vonderful part in your picture for me."

"Sure is, honey," I said. "We'll have it written tomorrow."

Panama and Frank devised a scene in which Zsa Zsa played a nurse who was trying to cure me of amnesia. She was to say, "I think I can get him to talk," then give me a big kiss.

Norman Panama, who was directing, ordered the scene to begin. Zsa Zsa gave me the kiss, then silence.

"Cut!" Norman said. "Bob—you were supposed to say a line there!"

"I can't talk with one lip," I gulped. You should have heard the crew—I wished we had that big a laugh in the picture.

Well, we did. It happened with a joke I was worried about. Peter Sellers did a one-day cameo as a doctor from India who also tried to cure me. At one point he asked me to read an eye chart in Hindi. When I said I couldn't, he replied, "I'll play it for you."

He picked up a reed instrument and started playing, using the chart for sheet music. A snake appeared and he charmed it. Afterward, I asked him what he would do if the snake bit him.

"Very simple," he said, "I simply cut the wound and suck out the poison."

"But what if it's in a place you can't reach with your mouth?" I asked.

"That," Peter replied, "is when you find out who your friends are."

I said to Norman and Mel: "You can't do that joke. It's based on a very well-known dirty story."

Panama and Frank insisted on trying. At the preview the joke got a full thirty-second laugh. The censors must have been laughing, too, because it stayed in the picture.

During *The Road to Hong Kong,* I was so eager to get on the golf links after work that I sometimes didn't have time to change my attire. One day I was doing the harem sequence, in which I was being adored by a bevy of dolls. One was even painting my toenails.

That afternoon I dashed off to the Wentworth club for a quick nine holes. Afterward I was discussing my game with a couple of Colonel Blimp types as I changed my clothes. I pulled off my spiked shoes and golf socks and gazed down in horror at my toenails, which looked like an Iceland sunset. The two club members saw the same sight and stared with open mouths. I tried to act debonair. It was one of my best performances.

Not long afterward, Bing and I were getting a hero's welcome in a *Road to Hong Kong* scene. That day I rushed to Wentworth again for another quick nine. I went to the locker room for a shower and nodded to a couple of dour gentlemen who were about to retire to the club room for their gin and bitters. As I peeled off my jockey shorts, a handful of confetti fell out.

The Road to Hong Kong

The Road to Hong Kong
(with Bing Crosby
and Peter Sellers)

I imagine that when the evenings get short at Wentworth, the members sit around a roaring fire and still talk about "that actor with the painted toenails and the confetti in his undergarments."

The *Call Me Bwana* caper began when Harry Saltzman called Mort Lachman from England. Harry Later discovered gold in England by co-producing the James Bond pictures, and he was associated with *The Iron Petticoat*. Mort is my head writer.

"I need a picture desperately," said Harry. "Is Bob available?"

"I don't know," Mort said. "Got a script?"

"I'll get one. I might do a safari story in Kenya."

Mort knows the way to my heart. He asked, "How far is it from the Mount Kenya Safari Club to the nearest golf course?"

"How should I know?" Harry asked.

"Find out and call me back."

Harry called back to say that the journey from the club to a golf

93

course took only twenty minutes by helicopter. "Then you might make a deal," Mort said.

Saltzman came to California with a script, which he showed to Mort before he brought it to me. "It's terrible," Mort said. "You can't show that to Bob."

"What can I do?" said Harry. "I've got to make a picture."

"Tell Bob how close it will be to the golf course and tell him you'll have the script ready in time," Mort suggested.

That's the way movie deals are made. Harry Saltzman did finally produce a script for *Call Me Bwana*, then disaster struck. The natives in Kenya became more than restless; they started killing people. Even with the nearness of the golf course, it didn't sound like a fun location to me. I had risked my life enough in vaudeville.

So we ended up filming *Call Me Bwana* at Pinewood Studios in England. The forest behind the studio doubled for the African

94

jungle. The weather was so cold that you could see the natives' breaths.

Gordon Douglas, the director of *Call Me Bwana*, staged one scene with me inside a cage with an ostrich. The animal started giving me the beady eye, and I knew I was in for trouble. He started beating on my head with his beak.

"What's the matter with this bird?" I yelled. "Did he see my last picture?"

My agent, Doc Shurr, was watching the scene, and he became very upset. "What are they doing to us!" he screamed.

"Doing to *us*?" I said. "Get in here and take 10 per cent of this!"

Call Me Bwana

IMPRESSIONS

In those early Paramount days, the studio press agents came up with imaginative ways to get the contract players in print. Here are some scenes Shirley Ross and I did during *Thanks for the Memory*. We were supposed to be discussing the styles of leading movie directors, then we acted out our impressions.

William Wellman, famed for his screwball comedies (*Nothing Sacred*).

Josef von Sternberg, who specialized in the exotic (*Morocco*).

Cecil B. De Mille, the man who glamorized the bathtub.

Frank Lloyd, master of the historical romance (*If I Were King*).

Frank Borzage, noted for his realism (*The Big City*).

Mitchell Leisen, whose films were marked by sophistication (*Midnight*).

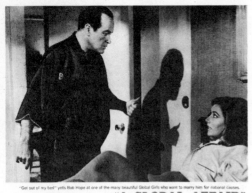

"Get out of my bed," yells Bob Hope at one of the many beautiful Global Girls who want to marry him for national causes.

METRO-GOLDWYN-MAYER presents "A GLOBAL AFFAIR"
A SEVEN ARTS-HALL BARTLETT PRODUCTION
Copyright © 1964 Metro-Goldwyn-Mayer Inc.   Printed in U.S.A.

A Global Affair is another example of how the best-laid plans, etc.

Ray Stark, who was producing films for Seven Arts, sold me on the idea of a baby who is abandoned at the United Nations in my care. It becomes an international issue, and ladies of several nations try to win my favor.

"We'll have an all-star cast of the world's greatest beauties," Ray enthused. "We'll get Sophia Loren from Italy, Brigitte Bardot from France—"

"You can stop right there, Ray," I said. "I'm sold."

That was the last I saw of him. Kim Novak was having problems on *Of Human Bondage,* another of Ray's pictures, and he disappeared into Ireland.

The casting didn't turn out the way Ray had described it. But one bit of casting did—Adlai Stevenson playing himself as American delegate to the United Nations. He just did a walk-on, but you'd think he had an Academy Award role.

"How do you think I look?" he asked me. "Are these blue pants okay? How much makeup should I wear?"

Again I was impressed with the similarity between actors and politicians.

A Global Affair
(with Adlai Stevenson)

I'll Take Sweden (with Frankie Avalon and Tuesday Weld)

Boy, Did I Get a Wrong Number!
(with Elke Sommer
and Phyllis Diller)

In *Boy, Did I Get a Wrong Number!* my co-stars were Elke Sommer and Phyllis Diller. Imagine making a movie with the Dish and the Crock.

We had to pay Phyllis a lot of money for the picture. She needed it. Her makeup man got stunt pay.

I can write those things about Phyllis because she knows how I feel about her. I think she's great. I'll never forget the first time I saw her perform in person. I happened to be in Washington, D.C., when I read that she was appearing at a place called the Lotus Club. I had seen her on the Jack Paar show and liked her raucous comedy. So I dropped by to see her.

The Lotus Club wasn't exactly jammed. When I arrived, the place looked like a two-table bridge tournament. The star act was a girl who billed herself as the Irish Señorita. Then came Phyllis Diller, the Twiggy of the Twilight Zone.

I knew what she was up against. I played enough of those supper shows on the Orpheum Circuit when my only audience was the ushers and a few salesmen waiting for the next train out of town. Phyllis did the best she could under the circumstances.

She tried to sneak out of the place, but I caught her going around a post. She was horrified when she recognized me. "Oh, my God, you didn't!" she exclaimed.

"Yes, I did," I replied. "And you were great!"

Later we began doing shows together, and she seemed a natural for *Boy, Did I Get a Wrong Number!* It was her first picture. When we did our first scene together, I noticed she was gazing all around the set.

"What are you looking for?" I asked.

"The cue cards," she said. "Where are the cue cards?"

"Phyllis, we don't use cue cards in movies," I said. "That's only in television."

"Oh?" she said. "Then I'd better learn my lines, huh?"

She learned plenty, and she did two other pictures with me—*Eight on the Lam* and *The Private Navy of Sgt. O'Farrell.*

Finally, a few words about two of my latest pictures (you'll note that actors never refer to "my last picture"—it's liable to be).

How to Commit Marriage was fun to make, even though I was working with two scene stealers. Every time the camera rolled, Jane Wyman rolled her big eyes, and Jackie Gleason rolled his big "A."

Ben Starr and Michael Kanin had written a generation-gap

Eight on the Lam
(with Phyllis Diller)

story they had intended for Cary Grant (how come I always get his rejects?). After they sent the script to me, I carried it around in my briefcase for a year and a half. Then one day in Paris I had some extra time so I re-read it. I telephoned Ben and Mike and said I'd buy it.

Norman Panama did a rewrite and was set to direct the picture. The problem was casting the role of the other father, a pop record producer. We tried Peter Ustinov, but he was tied up with other pictures. It never occurred to me that Jackie Gleason was available. But Norm Panama ran into him at a party, and Jackie said he would be in Hollywood for the summer. He was then making *Skidoo* for Otto Preminger.

"Gleason? He'd be great," I told Norm. "Let's go for him."

Panama and my producer, Bill Lawrence, went to see Gleason in jail. No, he wasn't serving time; Preminger was shooting a

105

How to Commit Marriage
(with Jackie Gleason)

Skidoo sequence in the Lincoln Heights jail. "I'll go for it," Gleason said.

Like all of my recent pictures, *How to Commit Marriage* was made in partnership with NBC. This time we had a new releasing company, Cinerama. With Gleason in the picture, it had to be wide screen. Also color and 100 proof.

It was the first time I had ever worked with Jackie, and it was a real pleasure. He is a total professional and, like Bing, he isn't afraid to throw you a straight line now and then.

How to Commit Marriage was kind of a departure for me, the subject matter was more daring than any I had done before. Jane and I were getting a divorce, and that so shocked our daughter that she refused to marry her fiancé and they had a baby out of wedlock. It was sort of an X- and G-rated movie. That means it was suitable for dirty families.

I even had some fairly torrid love scenes with Maureen Arthur in the picture. At my stage in life, its comforting to have your love scenes on film.

Two years went by before I made another picture. The reason was not because I didn't have offers. I was going to play the title role in *The Love Machine*, but Ralph Nader had me recalled to the factory for faulty parts.

Cancel My Reservation came from a script I owned, *Broken Gun*. I had planned to produce it with another actor as star, but the deal didn't go through. Then Tom Sarnoff of NBC said, "Why don't you do *Broken Gun* yourself?"

Why not? The script was rewritten, and we shot most of the picture in Carefree, Arizona. It was a pleasure to work with Eva Marie Saint again; she had been my leading lady sixteen years before in *That Certain Feeling*.

My big thrill with *Cancel My Reservation* came when it was selected to play the biggest, most prestigious movie house in the world, the Radio City Music Hall. It was the first time that one of my pictures played there.

Now I've had everything in my movie career. Everything, that is, except the Oscar. They gave me one a few years ago, but I'm not sure what it was for. The engraving said, "Made in Japan." I've lost the Best Acting award so many times that they call me the Pagliacci of the TelePrompter. At my house when they talk about the Academy Awards they call it the Passover. Once I had my writers prepare me an acceptance speech. I don't remember

106

how long ago that was, but I do know that the speech is in Latin. One year I was so desperate that I told my producer, "Get me something I can go after an Academy Award with." He sent me a submachine gun. Maybe I should just give up the idea of trying to win an Oscar and just have Mickey Rooney bronzed.

I want you to know that I'm not bitter. Envious maybe. But I still am willing to appear on the Oscar telecast. The Jolly Green Emcee, they call me. It's still Hollywood's most exciting night of the year. When I appeared on the show in 1975, I hadn't felt so much electricity since I backed into Glen Campbell's guitar. Raquel Welch walked by and twelve envelopes steamed open.

The movies that have been nominated for Oscars in recent years have made life easier for my writers. Consider the disaster movies. I was watching *Earthquake* one night, and the man next to me squeezed my hand. "It's okay," he whispered, "I'm your insurance man." I went to see *The Poseidon Adventure* and I knew the ocean liner was going to turn over—I saw Shelley Winters running from rail to rail. Fred Astaire didn't dance in *The Towering Inferno*, but it wasn't noticeable—not with all that smoke pouring out of his shoes. I don't know why they pick Charlton Heston to save everybody in those disaster movies. When he was asked to carry some tablets down from the mountain, he dropped them.

Cancel My Reservation
(with Eva Marie Saint)

WHY I DIDN'T WIN THE OSCAR

The Road to Rio

How to Commit Marriage

Son of Paleface

My Favorite Blonde

Monsieur Beaucaire

Casanova's Big Night

My Favorite Spy

The Road to Bali

The Princess and the Pirate

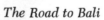

Alias Jesse James

Fancy Pants

The Godfather was so realistic that my popcorn started tasting like garlic. And I could almost feel my shoes turning to cement. I went to the premiere in Hollywood and saw all the stars being thrown out of speeding black limousines. After the picture was over I spent an hour sitting in my car in the parking lot; I was trying to get up the nerve to step on the starter. A passing car backfired, and everyone in the parking lot surrendered. *The Godfather* was such a hit that Paramount made *The Godfather, Part II*, giving us the rest of the horse.

The Exorcist was so scary that Vincent Price was afraid to see it. A theological student saw the movie and came out saying, "If that's what finals are like, I'm in big trouble." Audiences were so terrified that one theater put Kaopectate in the popcorn. I was surprised that *The Exorcist* won only two Oscars. One of the losers left the awards with his tail between his legs. I think the Academy regretted not giving the movie more Oscars. On the day after the awards, the president of the Academy turned into a frog.

I stayed home and watched the awards in 1976 on my television set—I saw the whole thing in green. I was surprised that *Jaws* didn't win, even though it has made more money than any movie in history. That's one mouth that even Howard Cosell envies. *Jaws* has cleared more beaches than the 1st Marine Division.

I was surprised that *Shampoo* was another loser. In that picture Warren Beatty had more going for him under the table than Lockheed. Lee Grant did win the supporting Oscar for her role in *Shampoo*, and what she said in the movie took the curl out of everyone's hair. I think Beatty should have had a share of her Oscar. He got a piece of everything else in the picture.

Jack Nicholson won the Best Actor award for *One Flew over the Cuckoo's Nest*. He played a man who's sane but pretends to be crazy. Just the opposite of the way most people act in Hollywood. Louise Fletcher won as Best Actress for her portrayal of the dedicated but cold nurse in *Cuckoo's Nest*. She was colder than a bedpan at the North Pole. I knew that George Burns was going to win as Best Supporting Actor in *The Sunshine Boys*. If they didn't give him the Oscar, he threatened to sing. George's victory did more for us senior citizens than anything since Geritol. Just my luck—old age is in, and my Grecian Formula won't wash out!

The movies have finally caught up with Oscar. Now they're both nude. Everyone is saying that Hollywood has changed. Not true. Hollywood has always been like that. They're just filming it now, that's all. I'd never work in those skin flicks. I don't need the exposure. I can remember when a director said, "Gimme some skin" and only wanted to shake hands. And when a "movie score" meant the music. Along with the new permissiveness on the screen has come a big jump in admission prices. Now it costs more to watch than to participate. They're doing things on the screen that I wouldn't do in bed . . . given the chance.

But that's enough of the one-liners. Have you ever noticed that I generally make jokes about people and things I really care about, whether the subject is a President, the United States, golf or Bing Crosby? The same is true of the movies. I may kid about sex on the screen or the antics of the stars, but the naked truth is that I'm awfully proud to have been part of the movie industry all these years.

I realize the power of Hollywood every time I take a trip overseas. I can be walking down the streets of Manila or Paris and some kid will take a glance at the ski nose and holler the local equivalent of "Hey—there's Bob Hope!"

For more than half a century, Hollywood has been exporting pleasure to the rest of the world. And not only pleasure, but spectacles that stir human emotion and dramas that dig deep into the human soul. Although some of the New Cinema appalls me, I think the change has generally been healthy.

Never again will Hollywood be accused of depicting a "lollypop" world. Critics claim there has been an excess of violence on the screen. Maybe so. But perhaps by showing the evil destruction of violence, movies can help cool it. More and more movies have explored the broad spectrum of human experience, delving into areas once considered taboo. Such films have shocked many people but they have also caused millions of others to talk out on problems once whispered about.

Hollywood speaks a universal language, and the neighborhood movie house is in a sense a meeting place for all the people. They laugh at the same silliness, hiss the same villains. They look at a mirror that is held up to nature. When they walk out of the darkened theater and into the light, they often have a better view of the world and of themselves.

I'm glad I took that Road to Hollywood. And before I quit, I'd like to take one more *Road*. Of course it will have to be downhill so Bing can make it.

HOW THE HOPE CHARM

Hedy Lamarr, *My Favorite Spy*

Eva Marie Saint, *That Certain Feeling*

WORKED ON MY LEADING LADIES

Joan Collins, *The Road to Hong Kong*

Milly Vitale, *The Seven Little Foys*

Andrea King, *the Lemon Drop Kid*

Virginia Mayo, *The Princess and the Pirate*

Joan Fontaine, *Casanova's Big Night*

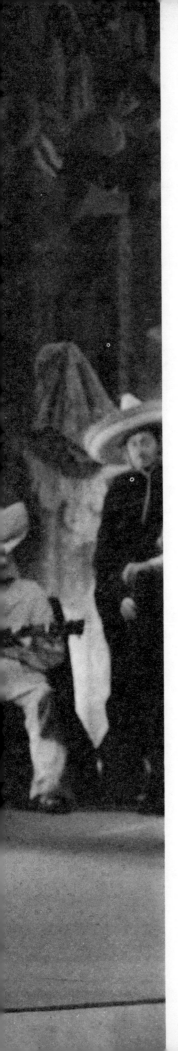

HOPE ON FILM
A Survey by Bob Thomas

The verbal comedian has not fared well at the hands of film critic-historians. The tone was set by the first of the important movie critics, James Agee, in his famous essay "Comedy's Greatest Era," which appeared in *Life* magazine September 3, 1949. Agee rhapsodized over four comics who did most of their work in silent films: Charles Chaplin, Buster Keaton, Harold Lloyd, Harry Langdon. Agee's praise was richly deserved, although Langdon's limited career scarcely qualified him for such swift company.

Agee could find little comedy to admire after the movies learned to talk. He wrote in *Life* magazine:

> Good comedy, and some that was better than good, outlived silence, but there has been less and less of it. The talkies brought one great comedian, the late majestically lethargic W. C. Fields, who could not possibly have worked as well in silence; he was the toughest and most warmly human of all screen comedians, and *It's a Gift* and *The Bank Dick*, fiendishly funny and incisive white-collar comedies, rank among the best comedies (and best movies) ever made. Laurel and Hardy, the only comedians who managed to preserve much of the large, low style of silence and who began to explore the comedy of sound, have made nothing since 1945. Walt Disney, at his best an inspired comic inventor and teller of fairy stories, lost his stride during the war and has since regained it only at moments. Preston Sturges made brilliant, satirical comedies, but his pictures are smart, nervous comedy-dramas merely italicized by slapstick. The Marx Brothers were side-splitters but they made their best comedies years ago. Jimmy Durante is mainly a nightclub genius; Abbott and Costello are semiskilled laborers, at best; Bob Hope is a good

The Big Broadcast of 1938 (with Ben Blue)

radio comedian with a pleasing presence, but not much more, on the screen.

Subsequent critics have followed the Agee line. It is unquestionably true that movie comedy reached a high point of development in the silent film. The early comedians, with their legions of gag men attempted to pile topper onto topper to maintain and build the audience's risibility. The result was blissful, inventive pantomime.

Lamentably, the great comedians did not survive the advent of sound (Chaplin continued making films that were largely silent; when he attempted much talk, he failed). After 1929, audiences welcomed a new kind of comedy, one that combined movement with dialogue, as well as music. Silent comedy had been a glorious interlude in the history of the performing arts. It might never have happened if the early films had talked as well as moved.

There could be no turning back to silent comedy. That dream world—necessarily unreal because the audience was deaf—gave way to a heightened sense of reality. Characters now talked and acted more like human beings, rather than performers in an antic ballet. Innocence had been lost. It could never be regained.

Something else was added. Dialogue provided a more contemporary air to screen comedy. Movies were built around subjects of the moment—Prohibition, the Depression, national conscription, etc.—and the jokes were phrased in the jargon of the day. That brought the immediate laughter of recognition (and also caused some of the films to date after a passage of years). Silent comedy may have been more sublime. Sound comedy got closer to the people.

The sound era has brought a host of able comedians, from Groucho Marx to Woody Allen. None has been more enduring than Bob Hope.

He came to Hollywood in 1937 with suitable, but not overwhelming, credentials. Like many entertainers of the period, he had been schooled in vaudeville, first as a dancer, then as a comedian. His easy elegance suited him for Broadway musicals, and he co-starred in several during the early 1930s. He tried radio, with no great success.

His Paramount bosses were slow to realize his potential. That may have been partly due to the fact that Paramount, unlike most of the other major studios, had no strong, permanent head of production. Also, the Hope talent was not immediately discernible. He was a good dancer, but no Astaire. He had a light, pleasant singing voice. Physically, he lacked the obvious comedic aspects of Groucho Marx or Joe E. Brown. Well, the nose. It did curve like a scimitar, but it wasn't an outrageous prop, like Jimmy Durante's.

What could be done with him? Paramount didn't discover until Hope had been under contract for a couple of years.

Bob Hope became the most serviceable of comedians. He could handle topical comedies or period farce, musical comedies or comedy adventures. As his career matured, he showed that he could sublimate the familiar Hope characteristics and play roles of dimension.

No comedian handles lines better. After his years in vaudeville and radio, he could find his way through the most labyrinthine of sentences, maintaining the sense of it and punching across the nonsense. He perfected a double take; unlike other comedians', his is verbal. When he is notified of some calamitous event, he continues his rapid chatter until the realization hits him:

"Excuse me, sir, but your coat's on fire."

"Yeah, well, if you hadn't been playing with matches—my WHAT?"

Hope's ability as a pantomimist has been underestimated by many critics—and by himself. One of his directors, Frank Tashlin, remarked: "Bob considered himself a talking comedian; he didn't feel comfortable in pantomime. When I suggested some broad comedy, he complained, 'Who do you think I am—Abbott and Costello?' Once I convinced him to try it, he performed beautifully. He has a dancer's grace, and he can move as well as any of the great pantomimists."

Another of Hope's directors, David Butler, agreed: "Bob relied too much on gags. My forte was pantomime; I had played in silent comedies myself. When we came to a bit of comedy action, he'd say, 'Show me how, show me how.' I'd demonstrate it for him, then he'd repeat it—much better than I."

Hope can mug with the best of comics, as he demonstrates in *The Road to Morocco* when he is posing as a statue to hide from the villains. A fly lands on his nose and he goes through facial contortions to get rid of it. Again, in *My Favorite Spy* he performs a musical number while under the influence of a truth serum. As the villains watch helplessly, he assumes the guises of Cyrano, Hamlet, and Jekyll-Hyde. It is a brilliant piece of miming.

Unlike most of the other great film comedians, Hope's career has not been limited to playing a single character. His versatility as an acting comedian has been proved again and again. But one character did persist. It was described by Frank Tashlin, who understood the Hope style as well as any director:

"All comedy is derivative; it draws from what has gone before. Bob's walk derived from that enormously inventive comic, Ted Healy, as did Jack Benny's and Ken Murray's. Bob drew his character from the timid fellows of Harold Lloyd, Buster Keaton, and Harry Langdon. But he added a new dimension: braggadocio.

"Bob uses his brashness to cover fear. The formula is simple: 1. the villain threatens Bob; 2. Bob responds with a challenge; 3. the villain pulls a gun; 4. Bob dissolves. There is a startling similarity between Bob and Donald Duck. Both became immensely popular during World War II. Both were braggers who backed down in a pinch but somehow prevailed."

We shall see the variations on the Hope style in a review of his films, from 1937 to 1972. For purposes of this survey, I have classified the Hope films in six categories: The Character Comedies, The Comedy Adventures, The *Roads*, The Farces, The Comedies of Character, and The Domestic Comedies. The reader may observe that some of the Hope films seem to fit two categories. It's possible. *Monsieur Beaucaire* may appear to be both a farce and a comedy adventure; it seemed to me that its adventure elements were pre-eminent.

Why no musical category? Although many of the Hope films contained songs and a few had production numbers, he seems to have made no out-and-out musical. *Here Come the Girls* comes the closest, but it has more of the aspect of a farce. Even when Paramount filmed a Broadway musical, *Louisiana Purchase*, the Irving Berlin score was subordinated to the comedy—and Hope was not given a single song.

It is interesting to ponder what might have happened if Bob Hope had been signed at M-G-M instead of Paramount. Probably he would have starred in a succession of glittering musicals, in which M-G-M was expert. Although Paramount made movies with songs, notably with Bing Crosby, it was not the musical factory that M-G-M became in the late 1930s and through the 1940s.

Paramount, the home of Ernst Lubitsch, the Marx Brothers, Mae West, Leo McCarey, W. C. Fields, Preston Sturges, and other masters of the sound comedy, was precisely the right place for Bob Hope.

The Character Comedies

Movie bosses have not been noted for their senses of humor. It is perhaps understandable that the Paramount executives had no real notion of what to do with a breezy young comedian from Broadway named Bob Hope. He came west with a reputation as a star of Broadway musicals and as a joke-teller on radio, but there was no way to relate him to the past, as was the Hollywood custom. Each new femme fatale was another Garbo, each new romantic star another Valentino. Bob Hope couldn't be compared with Chaplin or Lloyd or any of the comics who came before.

Paramount initially cast Hope in a series of roles that might have been written for any other light-comedy actor; indeed, his first part had been designed for Jack Benny. In the next five films he also played characters that do not appear to have been written with Hope's special talents in mind; rather they were standard characters from standard scripts.

First came *The Big Broadcast of 1938*. It was no worse than the three *Big Broadcasts* that had preceded it; in fact, it may have been better, because of the presence of W. C. Fields. Inevitably, Fields dominated the film with his monumental illogic, drawing from most of his standard routines. He even manages to inject a golf game that has no relation to the rest of the film. When he has milked the routine, Fields converts his golf cart into a tiny airplane and joins the rest of the cast on an ocean liner embarked upon a transatlantic race. Madness.

Despite Hope's billing—sixth, between Lynne Overman and Ben Blue—he plays an important role in the film, appearing almost as much as Fields. For his opening scene in his first feature, Hope is in jail. His three ex-wives taunt him from outside the bars for his inability to pay their alimony. One of them, Shirley Ross, is more sympathetic toward him than the other two. Hope's fiancée,

123

College Swing
(with Martha Raye)

Dorothy Lamour, arrives to pay the bail after hocking her engagement ring, which he admits is not paid for. All ship aboard the S.S. *Colossal;* Hope, a disc jockey, is supposed to broadcast bulletins on the race with another liner.

Hope plays emcee for the ship's entertainment, which ranges from Tito Guizar to Kirsten Flagstad. He strides onstage with the now familiar Hope walk and tosses off jokes that are purposely bad ("Here's the one about the man who went to the dentist; he only had a dollar so they gave him buck teeth"). He never loses his earnest air, even when gliding through a ballroom dance with Shirley Ross in the production number "The Waltz Lives On."

One sequence possesses a hint of reality in the concocted *Big Broadcast of 1938.* That comes when Hope and Ross sit at the ship's bar and contemplate their drinks with bittersweet sentiment. All the small pleasures of a ruined marriage are recalled as they alternate the lines of "Thanks for the Memory." Then the poignant moment is over, and the nonsense continues.

With Hope's second film, *College Swing* (1938), the billing improved (fourth), but the role worsened. This time he plays the rather undefined role of a manager who schemes to coach Gracie Allen in examinations which would determine whether or not she inherits a college. Hope's lines are largely limited to wisecracks such as when he remarks to the college president: "You'd better answer your phone." When the president, played by Charles Trowbridge, protests that the telephone isn't ringing, Hope answers, "It's silly to wait for the last minute." (The Paramount writers so enjoyed this line that it shows up later in *Nothing but the Truth.*)

In *College Swing*, as in three of the other Character Comedies, Hope appears with Martha Raye, Paramount's resident comedienne. The pairing provides a lively duet, "How'dja Like to Love Me?"

After a clinch, Raye says, "That kiss took a lot out of you, huh?"

"Why not?" answers Hope. "You kiss like a vacuum cleaner."

The dialogue is much the same in *Give Me a Sailor* (1938). The plot was obviously designed to exploit the ugly-duckling qualities of Martha Raye. She plays the workhorse sister of frivolous, flighty Betty Grable. Both are in love with a Navy lieutenant and the paper-thin plot revolves around their efforts to snag him. Hope, unconvincingly cast as Jack Whiting's ensign brother, is co-conspirator. His favorite exclamation: "Great Caesar's ghost!"

The Hope-Raye pairing works better in *Never Say Die* (1939). The setting is one of those wacky mythical places which abounded in the Paramount gazetteer (*Duck Soup, Million Dollar Legs*, etc.). Hope is a millionaire hypochondriac who comes to Bad Gaswatter for a cure. His condition allows Hope to sneak in one of his favorite gags from vaudeville. He starts jiggling after taking medicine, and his butler, Ernest Cossart, asks if he has the chills. "No, I forgot to shake the bottle," says Hope.

Never Say Die profits from a wry script by Don Hartman, Frank Butler, and Preston Sturges and the feathery direction of Elliott Nugent. The supporting cast is first-rate: Gale Sondergaard as the fortune-seeking vamp, who happens to be an Olympic pistol shot; Andy Devine as Martha Raye's Texas boy friend; Alan Mowbray as an impoverished nobleman; Christian Rub as the town mayor; Monty Woolley in a bit as the doctor who mistakenly diagnoses Hope's fatal illness.

Amusing though it is, *Never Say Die* fails to exploit Hope's own comic nature, fitting him instead into a script-tailored character. It is an essentially weak character, since most of the time he thinks he is sick or dying.

The other two Character Comedies were efforts to capitalize on the Bob Hope-Shirley Ross teaming which had worked well in *The Big Broadcast of 1938. Thanks for the Memory* (1938) portrays them more or less as the couple in the song. The film is notable for the introduction of a Frank Loesser-Hoagy Carmichael standard, "Two Sleepy People."

Bob Hope considers *Some Like It Hot* (1939) to be the nadir of his feature-film career. It's not as bad as all that. There are some good moments, especially in the relationship between Hope and Shirley Ross. But the comedy is lame, and the character written for Hope could have been played by any glib-talking actor, from Lee Tracy to Pat O'Brien.

The Character Comedies were a prelude to the films that would truly portray the Hope personality. Perhaps it was a necessary interval, to acquaint him with the film medium and to introduce movie audiences to him. Also to convince the Paramount bosses that they had to tailor film roles to the unique Hope personality, rather than force him into preconceived characters.

The Comedy Adventures

The line between farce and comedy adventure is very fine indeed, but it must be drawn here for purposes of analysis. Farce aims at the follies and foibles of human nature; its tradition ranges from Plautus to Molière to the raucous sketches of old-time burlesque houses. Comedy adventure, as practiced by Bob Hope, is often farcical in nature, but its roots are basically cinematic: the Western, the thriller, the swashbuckler, and other standard forms of film entertainment.

The best example is Hope's most successful film financially— *The Paleface* (1948).

The film makers were careful not to poke fun at the Western. Burlesque Westerns have rarely succeeded, perhaps because Western fans do not enjoy having their values ridiculed. *The Paleface* employs all the basic elements of the Western—chases, gun duels, slugfests, Indian fights, the sharp contrast between good and evil—without deriding them. Those elements are switched for comedy purposes.

The most inspired switch proves to be the situation of having the female lead—Jane Russell as Calamity Jane—perform the heroics, while Hope plays a cautious dentist who is deceived into bravery. It is an appealing situation with endless comic possibilities. Russell plays it straight throughout, as do the villains, thus lending credibility to the tale.

The Paleface is filled with funny sequences: Hope administering laughing gas to a burly miner; Hope posing as a cadaver in the undertaker's parlor while the villains load dynamite into caskets; Hope and a desperado stalking in *High Noon* style but being unable to find each other.

The madness continues to the end. The townspeople give the newlyweds a send-off. Russell snaps the reins, and the horses drag

127

The Paleface (with Jane Russell)

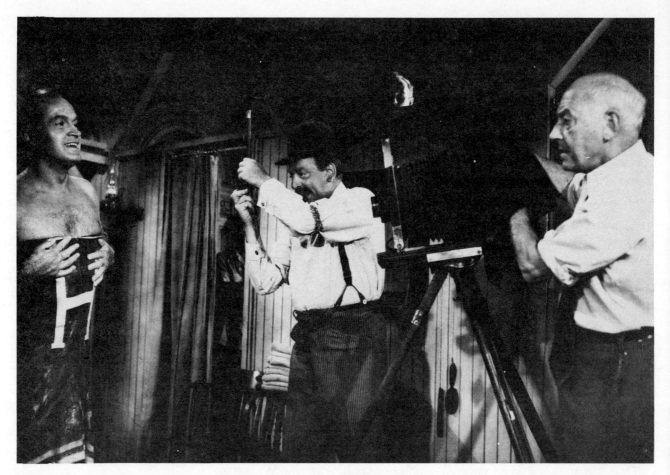

Son of Paleface
(with Robert Welch
and Cecil B. De Mille)

her off the wagon. Alone in the wagon, Hope stares at the audience and says, "What do you want—a happy ending?"

Like most film sequels, *Son of Paleface* (1952) did not equal the original, but it had its moments. Again teamed with Jane Russell, Hope this time portrays the son of Painless Potter, a Harvard graduate who goes out West to claim his inheritance. Roy Rogers joins the cast as a federal agent.

Son of Paleface is notable for the sight gags of Frank Tashlin: Hope shoots a stuffed moose which pours forth coins like a Las Vegas jackpot; Hope throws banana peels to fell pursuing Indians; Hope uses a rope to hold up the disabled fourth wheel of his racing automobile and pleads with the rescuing Rogers: "Hurry up—this is unbelievable."

When a photographer arrives to take a picture of Hope in a bathtub, Hope says, "Hurry up; who do you think you are—Cecil B. De Mille?" It is Cecil B. De Mille.

Alias Jesse James (1959) again casts Hope as the loser—this time a New York insurance man whose sales record descends off the chart. But then he sells a $100,000 policy to a visitor from Mis-

128

souri who admits to being "well-known in railroad and banking circles." Jesse James.

The premise sets up an ideal vehicle for Hope's talents. He is sent West to retrieve the policy or guard James's health, lest the insurance company face bankruptcy. His jeopardy is demonstrated as soon as he arrives in Angel's Rest, Missouri. In quick succession he: is forced to take a slug of whiskey which causes smoke to pour from his ears; sells an insurance policy to a prospector who is then shot to death; is tricked into a poker game; has his four kings eaten by a goat; is stripped to his long red underwear by the gamblers; blunders into the boudoir of the dance-hall singer, Rhonda Fleming, mistress of Jesse James.

Norman McLeod keeps the sight gags coming, and it is perhaps Hope's most physical comedy. The funniest business comes when Hope substitutes for James (Wendell Corey) in a gun duel with a visiting desperado. Hope turns out the winner because of a device which fires his guns when he lifts his hat.

There is a chase in the best silent-film tradition, with Hope running inside a floorless wagon while Fleming drives the horses. The final shoot-out is reminiscent of *The Paleface*. But instead of Jane

Alias Jesse James

Alias Jesse James

My Favorite Spy
(with Hedy Lamarr)

Russell doing the shooting for Hope, he has the help of a pack of television gunslingers—Hugh O'Brian, Ward Bond, James Arness, Roy Rogers, Gail Davis, and Jay Silverheels—as well as Gary Cooper ("Yup") and Bing Crosby ("This fellow needs all the help he can get").

The theme of mistaken identity figures in nearly all of the Comedy Adventures. It is sure-fire. Hope first appears as one of life's losers, a tailor or a burlesque comic. By accident he is thrust into a world of high politics and deadly intrigue, peopled with dangerous villains and desirable women. He hurtles from one hazardous situation to another, surviving mostly by chance.

The mistaken identity theme affords an endless variety of comic situations. It also holds enormous audience appeal in providing Walter Mitty dreams for the ordinary citizen.

The gimmick worked well in the spy pictures. In *My Favorite Spy* (1951) Hope is Peanuts "Boffo" White, a hokey burlesque comic who bears an uncanny resemblance to a superspy, Eric Augustine. Government agents kill the spy by error, and Peanuts is enlisted to take his place on a hazardous mission.

"That ain't my line of work," Hope protests. "I tell jokes. That's dangerous enough."

Hope resists until he receives a call from the White House. "How is Margaret?" he asks. "Oh—she's on tour? . . . Well, that always was a tough town to play."

Truman's call convinces Hope, and he submits to a brainwashing to convert him to the suave Augustine. Much of the comedy derives from his inability to maintain the masquerade. Norman McLeod helps sustain the illusion by quickening the pace, ending with a Mack Sennett chase that features Hedy Lamarr at the wheel of a runaway fire truck. As he dangles from the ladder, Hope comments, "If I saw this on television, I wouldn't believe it." On the big screen, the mad proceedings are surprisingly convincing.

In *My Favorite Blonde* (1942), Hope is the lesser half of the vaudeville team of Haines and Percy, the latter a talented penguin. Fleeing from murderous spies, British agent Madeleine Carroll encounters Hope backstage and embarks on a cross-country chase to Hollywood, where Percy has been contracted for a film, *Igloo Love*.

The flight is a slapstick *It Happened One Night*, with Hope and Carroll eluding the enemy agents and peace officers—Hope is falsely accused of murder—by bus, train, and airplane. The pace is

130

frantic, and the sight gags are profuse, but credibility is enhanced by the straightforward playing of the serenely beautiful Madeleine Carroll. (Hope always seems to be menaced by George Zucco or Gale Sondergaard; in *Blonde,* he is subjected to both.)

Where There's Life (1947) opens with an assassination attempt on the king of a mythical European country. The chief general, Signe Hasso, goes to New York to find the king's heir, his son by a secret American marriage. He is also sought by a murderous gang of revolutionists.

Again, Hope is a normal, non-hero type who is catapulted into danger. He is a radio disc jockey for Barko dog food, engaged for eight years to the sister of New York cop William Bendix ("We've been looking for an apartment," Hope explains).

Bendix's innate distrust of his sister's longtime fiancé becomes compounded when Hope tries to explain that he is the king of a European nation and is being pursued by a pack of cutthroats. Hope also has trouble accounting for the presence in his bedroom of a lovely woman he claims to be a general assigned to his protection.

My Favorite Brunette (1947) opens with Hope on Death Row in San Quentin prison. "No ketchup?" he complains. "This is the worst last meal I ever had." He inquires whether the governor has sent a commutation of his death sentence. "No word, huh?" he shrugs. "Well, I'll know who to vote for next time."

Hope greets reporters and tells in flashback how he got into his predicament. The rest is an amiable travesty on the private-eye films that were prevalent in the postwar years. Hope is a baby photographer who is mistaken for the private investigator in the next office—Alan Ladd in an amusing walk-on.

When Dorothy Lamour enlists his aid against a gang of plotters, Hope assumes the private-eye role. He adopts the wide-lapelled trench coat, snap-brim hat, and stolid manner. But when he snaps open his pistol, the bullets fall to the floor. "Small bullets," he reasons.

Hope has a new set of adversaries: Peter Lorre, Charles Dingle, John Hoyt, and Lon Chaney, Jr., in his Lennie Small character from *Of Mice and Men.* Hope and Lamour are on the run most of the time, and he escapes execution only at the fade-out. The disappointed executioner is Bing Crosby. "He'll take any kind of part," Hope remarks.

They Got Me Covered (1943) is a topical comedy full of references to wartime America. Hope is a discredited foreign corre-

My Favorite Brunette (with John Hoyt)

spondent flying home from Russia. He is asked if he is headed for a special destination. "No, I'm just keeping this seat warm for Mrs. Roosevelt," he says—a reference to the peripatetic First Lady. Hope explains how he muffed the story of Germany's invasion of Russia: "You can't trust that Hitler." A fellow passenger puts down his newspaper and says, "You're-a tellin' me!" He looks exactly like Mussolini.

That's the tenor of the film, which involves Hope and Dorothy Lamour with a pack of Axis spies headed by a classic team of villains: Otto Preminger as the Nazi, Eduardo Ciannelli as the Italian Fascist, and Philip Ahn as the Japanese.

David Butler keeps the pace furious, and the gag writers do the rest. The climax comes when Hope poses as a mannequin in a beauty salon which is the headquarters for the spy ring.

The swashbuckler proved an ideal medium for the Hope mistaken identity theme, supplying three of his most satisfying comedies.

Monsieur Beaucaire (1946) is a gem of insanity, portraying Hope as barber to the French court. He is hopelessly in love with the chambermaid, Joan Caulfield, and starts to hang himself. "But you didn't tie the rope," Leonid Kinskey observes. "I was just going to take a few practice swings," Hope responds.

His maladroitness as a barber provides some brilliant slapstick, as when he powders the wig of Louis XIV, Reginald Owen. George Marshall keeps a sure hand on the ribaldry as king, queen, Madame Pompadour, and her lover shuttle between bedrooms, abetted by Hope.

The comedy is compounded when Hope masquerades as ambassador to the Spanish court, eluding conspirators seeking to unmask him and cause war between France and Spain. Hope and chief plotter Joseph Schildkraut engage in a duel which is a brilliant takeoff on those of Errol Flynn. Schildkraut escapes, and the epilogue shows him shining shoes in the Philadelphia barbershop where Hope is ministering to George Washington.

The same materials are employed in *Casanova's Big Night* (1954), but with not quite the same exuberance. Still it is an amusing situation—Hope as a tailor posing in the guise of a debt-ridden Casanova—and the supporting cast is the best of all Hope films—Basil Rathbone, John Carradine, Arnold Moss, Hope Emerson, John Hoyt, Lon Chaney, Vincent Price unbilled as the errant Casanova, Frieda Inescort, Raymond Burr in a bit as a courtier. Hope has some funny scenes in his efforts to live up to

133

Monsieur Beaucaire (with Leonid Kinskey)

Casanova's reputation. The climactic duel with Hope dressed as a Venetian dowager is a delight.

As in many Hope films, there is an epilogue. Action is stopped just as the headsman's ax is descending on Hope's neck. An announcer says that is how Paramount planned to end the picture. An alternate ending as written, directed, and produced by "Bob (Orson Welles) Hope" shows him escaping the ax, skewering his enemies three at a time. Encircled by swordsmen, Hope ducks, and they wound each other. "Wasn't that better?" he asks the audience.

The Princess and the Pirate (1944) proves almost perfectly designed for Hope's talents, and he plays it with remarkable zest. He portrays a hapless actor called Sylvester the Great, the Man of Seven Faces (while removing his makeup, he says, "Wait a minute while I take off my putty nose," then discovers it's his own). He shows off his clippings to the disguised princess, Virginia Mayo, describing his triumphs in world capitals. "You should have seen me on the road to Morocco," he remarks, adding, "but some overage crooner with laryngitis crabbed my act."

Hope again enacts the devout coward, and he is harassed by an endless number of villains, especially Victor McLaglen, capital as the infamous Hook, and Walter Slezak, a corrupt grandee. Walter Brennan, toothless and cackling, plays the shrewd imbecile who steals McLaglen's map and tattoos it on Hope's chest. The circumstance provides a hilarious sequence in which Hope tries to conceal his chest while taking a sulphur bath with Slezak.

The funniest sequence comes when Hope disguises himself as Hook and begins blustering orders to the pirate crew. Then McLaglen appears to countermand the orders, confounding the pirates. David Butler directs the sequence for a maximum of laughs, climaxing it with a scene in which McLaglen tricks Hope into thinking he is looking at himself in the mirror. He soon discovers it is McLaglen's face he is staring at.

Even in his starring film, Hope loses to Crosby.

After rescue from the pirates, Virginia Mayo overlooks Hope to choose her commoner husband, a seaman who turns out to be Crosby. "How do you like that!" Hope protests. "I knock my brains out for nine reels and some bit player from Paramount comes over and gets the girl! This is the last picture *I* make for Goldwyn!" Curiously, it was.

Early in his film career, Bob Hope appeared in two comedy thrillers. Both co-starred Paulette Goddard, whose vivacity and

Casanova's Big Night (with Joan Caulfield and Arnold Moss)

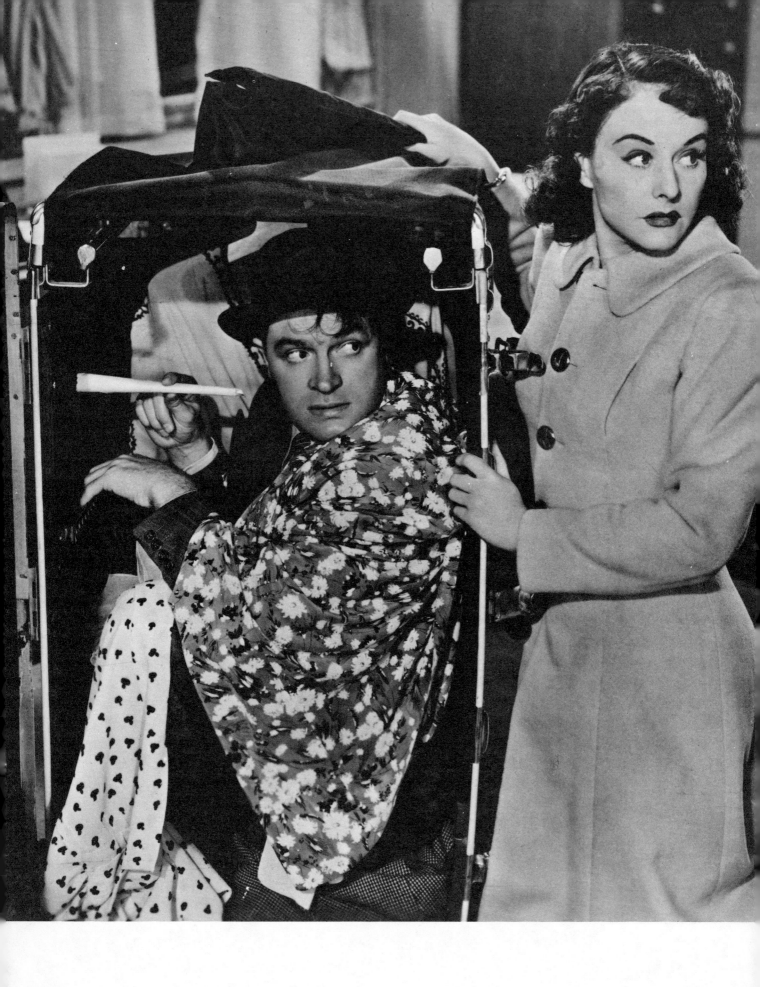

screaming power made her ideal for the assignments. Both films succeeded as popular entertainments.

The Cat and the Canary (1939) was an updating of the old stage and silent-film melodrama. Elliott Nugent and the authors, Walter De Leon and Lynn Starling, played it for laughs, which is the best way to treat the familiar formula of heirs being eliminated one by one in a creaky old mansion. The action was timed with skill, moving from one plateau to the next higher one. The first major film tailored to the talents of Bob Hope, it was crucial to his career.

The Ghost Breakers (1940), which followed the first *Road* picture, helped consolidate Hope's popularity with film audiences. It is ideally constructed, with Hope, ably assisted by Willie Best, providing comedy to relieve the growing tension.

The film opens during a power blackout in New York City (prophetic?). George Marshall establishes the mood at once with candlelight and a lightning storm. Paulette Goddard is determined to take possession of her family's Cuban mansion despite warning that "in the last twenty years no human being has slept there overnight and lived." Hope is a Winchell-like newsman on radio who gets in trouble with mobsters, believes mistakenly that he has committed a murder, and seeks escape. He manages it by hiding in the steamer trunk of Goddard. One of the film's funniest scenes comes when Willie Best is conversing with Hope, who is inside the trunk at dockside. Along bumbles Jack Norton, Hollywood's eternal drunk, who believes Best to be a clever ventriloquist.

During the night in the mansion, Marshall executes every possible trick of the haunted-house movie: a monstrous zombie on the loose; secret panels and clutching hands; an organ that plays mysteriously; skeletons and rising corpses; a suit of armor that starts to move; hidden passageways and buried treasure.

Also a ghost that rises from a tomb and floats through the halls. The ghost remains unexplained.

The Ghost Breakers (with Paulette Goddard)

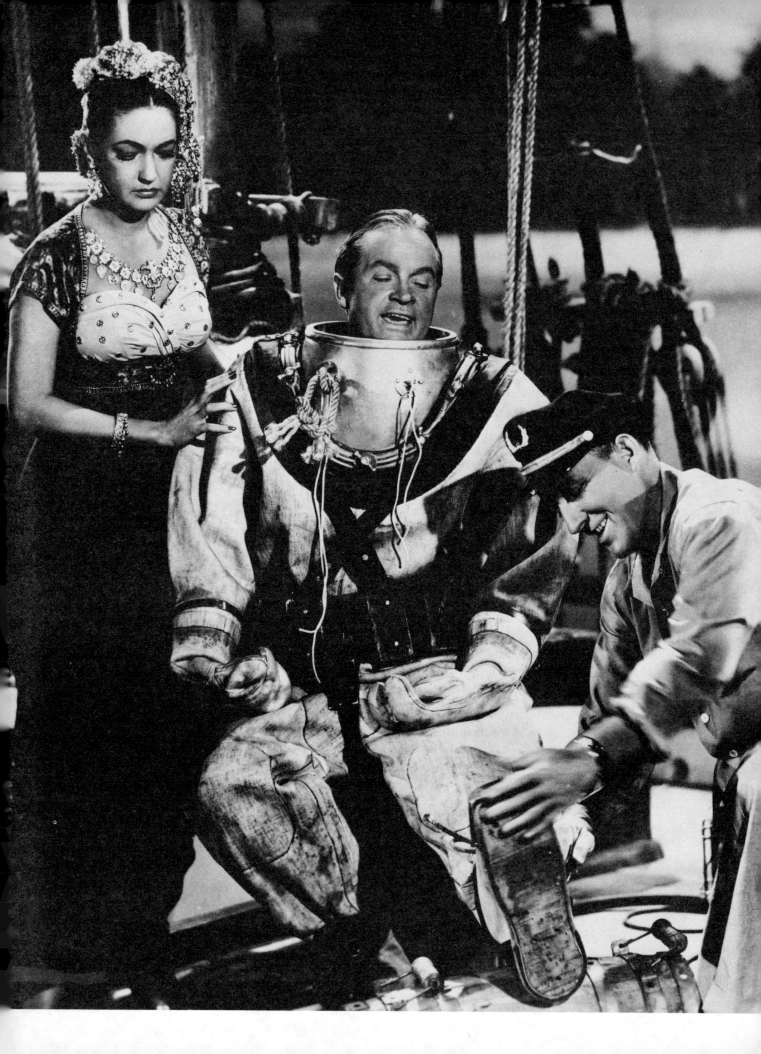

The *Roads*

Since the beginning of film history, the comedic art has been enriched by the pairing of two complementary talents. None has been more felicitous than the joining of Bob Hope and Bing Crosby in the seven *Road* films they made with Dorothy Lamour.

During the early 1940s, the Paramount writing department was blessed by another pair of blithe talents, Frank Butler and Don Hartman. They created the screenplays of the first three *Roads*—*Singapore*, *Zanzibar*, and *Morocco*. Whether by design or accident, they happened upon a formula that was simple yet sure-fire: Crosby is the debonair adventurer with a bottomless bag of get-rich schemes; Hope is his trusting friend, with enough bravado to attempt such schemes, which usually turn out disastrously. Crosby is the romantic, insinuating love songs to the exotic Lamour; Hope has an adolescent's ambitions of amour, and often he appears close to his goal. But usually he walks into the sunset alone.

The Road to Bali demonstrates the extent of Hope's frustrations. In the final minutes, Lamour decides that she wants to spend her life with Crosby. The distraught Hope attempts a trick that has worked before: he blows a reed instrument over a woven basket. The magic works once more; a voluptuous Jane Russell materializes. But Russell chooses Crosby, too, and Hope pleads, "What are you going to do with two girls?"

"That's my problem," Crosby answers airily. As he strolls off with two beauties, Hope struggles to keep the THE END sign from appearing on the screen. "This picture isn't over yet," he wails. "Call the producer . . . call the writers!" But he fails in his effort to stop the fade-out.

Crosby and Hope blend to perfection. Crosby has a master touch with the offhanded line; Hope can match him with banter

139

The Road to Bali

The Road to Singapore

and can handle the more physical comedy as well. Neither is dominant, as is the case with most teams of funnymen.

The pair had wider appeal than most comedians. Traditionally, comedians attracted a predominantly male audience. The *Road* pictures, with their themes of girl chasing as well as fortune hunting, appealed to both sexes. Both Crosby and Hope were attractive to women in ways that the broader comedians were not.

The success of the *Road* pictures was due to more than sex appeal. They were superb escapism in a time of war. Pure entertainments, they offered a depiction of a simpler, more adventurous way of life in which two companions of nerve and whimsy could toss conformism to the winds. Hope and Crosby were a modern Tom Sawyer and Huck Finn in search of adventure, but also with other things on their minds. Like sex, loot, and a hint of larceny.

Story construction of the *Roads* appears chaotic, but it has a design. The formula was described by Harry Tugend, who co-wrote the original story and produced *Bali:* "Get 'em up a tree; throw rocks at 'em; get 'em out of the tree."

Getting Hope and Crosby up the tree was simple; the script writers needed only a consummate villain like Anthony Quinn, Gale Sondergaard, Douglas Dumbrille, or Murvyn Vye to place the two heroes in jeopardy. Getting the pair down from the tree required no scripting miracles. The writers could resort to short cuts, as in *Bali.* Hope seeks treasure on the ocean floor in a diving suit, encounters a giant squid (a relic of *Reap the Wild Wind?*), is rescued when Crosby and Lamour inflate his suit by a shipboard pump. Villain Anthony Quinn fires bullets into the suit, but Hope isn't inside. He clambers over the side of the boat.

"How did you get out of that diving suit?" Crosby demands.

"It was easy," says Hope. He pantomimes a desperate struggle to Crosby. Crosby walks to the camera, shrugs, and the film continues.

The *Road* plan did not spring full-mapped from the Paramount film factory. The first of the films, *The Road to Singapore,* appeared in 1940 with no apparent predestination as a series. The plot was typical of prewar comedies in which Paramount was adept. Crosby is the son of shipping magnate Charles Coburn. Fed up with the stuffy life and his snobbish fiancée, he ships out to the South Pacific with a low-brow friend, Hope. They land in the mythical isle of Kaigoon, on their way to Singapore. (They never make it to Singapore, and such is their fate in the ensuing films: they never reach the end of the road.)

140

On Kaigoon, they rescue a native entertainer (Lamour) from the cruel Anthony Quinn. After a series of adventures, Crosby is claimed by his father and fiancée, and Hope leaves with Lamour. Crosby has second thoughts, and he escapes after a chance encounter with Hope. It turns out that Hope hasn't married Lamour. "You're the dopey-looking klutz she wants," he tells Crosby.

The Road to Singapore has a more articulated plot than the later *Roads,* but it lacks definition of the two leading characters. Crosby, as the wealthy shipping heir, plays his role more conservatively. Hope, the artless vagabond, is more the perpetrator of the outrageous schemes. In later films, Crosby becomes the provocateur, Hope the victim.

The basic inspirations are here. Hope and Crosby bat the witty lines back and forth like shuttlecocks. Their unique talents combine in rollicking musical numbers. They introduce the running gag of patty-caking prior to the start of a donnybrook.

The theme is anti-establishment. Crosby escapes the stuffed-shirt life to rove with Hope, a confirmed drifter. They are continually at odds with the authorities, because of unkept promises to local maidens or outrageous schemes to bilk the native population.

In *The Road to Zanzibar* (1941), all of the *Road* elements coalesce. The picture opens with Crosby singing "You Lucky People, You" to a gathering of yokels at a carnival. He is touting an attraction called Fearless Frazier, the Living Bullet. Fearless is Hope, unhappily stuffed into the muzzle of a cannon. "I don't mind being drafted, but not for ammunition," he complains.

He asks the blond assistant, "Where were you last night?"

"With my grandmother," she replies.

"Yeah? Well, your grandmother got in bed with me last night and he had lip rouge on his collar."

Crosby brings the crowd inside to witness the launching. The cannon fires and a projectile is flung into space. It's a dummy that hits a circus tent and begins a fire that destroys the entire carnival. The owner and his thugs set off in pursuit of Hope and Crosby, and the flight begins.

All the ingredients are established in the first few minutes: Crosby the schemer, Hope the victim; Crosby the lover, Hope the loser. Both involved in chicanery that causes them to be on the lam for the remainder of the picture. This sense of mobility is part of the genius of the *Roads.* Hope and Crosby are never in one place long enough for boredom to threaten. As soon as a locale is

The Road to Zanzibar

141

milked for its comic possibilities, the script writers send them on their way.

In *The Road to Zanzibar*, Hope and Crosby begin to depart from the ordinary confines of a script. They attempt their patty-cake routine on a hulking villain; he slugs them before they can complete it. "He must have seen the picture," Hope cracks. Aside from this reference to *The Road to Singapore*, nothing is outside the frame of the plot, and none of the action is supernatural.

That changed with *The Road to Morocco* (1942).

The two stars sing the title song as they travel the desert on camelback. They contemplate the adventures ahead: ". . . I'll lay you eight to five that we'll meet Dorothy Lamour . . . Paramount won't let anything happen to us—we're signed for five more years . . ."

When Hope starts explaining the plot, Crosby says, "I know that."

"Yeah, but the people who came in the middle of the picture don't," says Hope.

"You mean they missed my song!" says Crosby.

The Road to Zanzibar

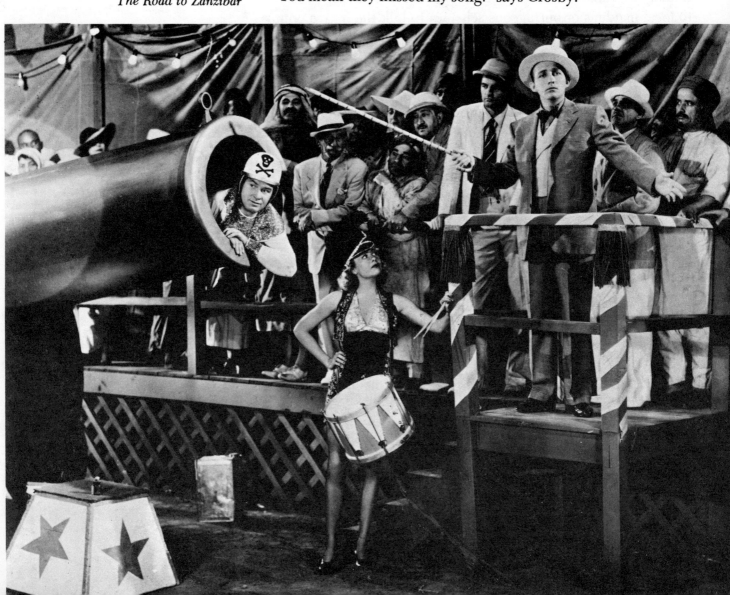

The authors discover the convenience of unraveling a *Road* plot when Hope asks how he and Crosby escaped from sacks in the middle of the desert.

Crosby: "If we told anybody, they'd never believe it."

Hope: "Okay, we won't tell."

Morocco is filled with outrageous sight gags directed by the veteran of silent comedy, David Butler. A camel mutters, "This is the screwiest picture I was ever in!" Hope discovers a magic ring and marvels, "Well, I'll be a monkey's uncle." He becomes one. Earlier, his curve-toed Arab shoes uncurl when Lamour kisses him. "Now kiss him on the nose," Crosby suggests; "see if you can straighten that out."

The Road to Utopia (1945) is the only period picture in the series. It begins with Lamour, Crosby, and Hope in old age, as they reminisce about their adventures in the Klondike at the turn of the century. Flashback. Despite some vintage costuming, the film has a contemporary air. When Hope and Crosby lose an amateur night contest, Hope mutters, "Next time I'll bring Sinatra." In the song "Put It There, Pal," they taunt each other about their flops, *Let's Face It* and *Mississippi*.

Utopia goes further with the device of gags and pieces of business outside the context of the plot. When Crosby arrives at his home, Hope complains, "And I thought this was going to be an A picture."

Crossing the arctic wastes by dogsled, the pair spy a familiar-looking mountain. "Bread and butter," Hope remarks. "That's a mountain," Crosby corrects. "Looks like bread and butter to me," Hope insists. The mountain assumes a halo of stars to duplicate the Paramount trademark.

When Hope and Crosby are stoking coal in a ship's boiler room, a man in a full-dress suit walks past. "Are you in this picture?" he is asked. "No, I'm just taking a short cut to Stage 10," he replies, continuing on his way.

The air of unreality is maintained by the periodic appearance of Robert Benchley in a circle at the corner of the screen. In mock-pedantic terms he explains what is happening: "This is a device known as a flashback."

Utopia was the first *Road* to be written by radio gag men, and more emphasis is placed on jokes, particularly of the nonsensical kind:

Hope: "Don't look at me! I didn't even want to get on this boat. I was Shangri-La-ed."

Crosby: "You mean shanghaied."

Hope: "Well, one of them towns in Egypt."

The Road to Rio (1948) mixes the familiar ingredients with more than usual zest. Again Bing and Bob are on the run from outraged fathers and brothers of susceptible beauties. Again they entertain the carnival audience with song and dance, and Hope's high-wire act sets fire to the whole spread. This time they escape by stowing away to South America.

Lamour is hypnotized into strange behavior by her avaricious aunt, Gale Sondergaard. "I find myself saying things and I don't know why I say them," Dorothy complains.

"Why don't you just run for Congress and forget about us?" says the exasperated Hope.

The finale is frantic and funny, with shots of Jerry Colonna leading the Brazilian cavalry to the rescue. It never arrives. "We never made it," Colonna shrugs. "Exciting, wasn't it?"

Rio was the first *Road* to make use of guest stars—the Andrews Sisters and the Wiere Brothers—and it appeared that the Paramount script department had run out of variations on the tripartite theme.

After a five-year lapse, *The Road to Bali* (1953) proved that the formula still worked. Color has been added for the first time, and it contributes immensely to the sense of exoticism and fantasy. Otherwise the mix is the same. The same heavy is back from *Singapore*—Anthony Quinn.

The madness continues. On one of their flights, Hope and Crosby make their way through a herd of sheep and start singing "The Whiffenpoof Song." The little lambs obligingly chorus, "Baa . . . baa . . . baa." Says Crosby: "Fred Waring must have played through here."

When Hope and Crosby are surrounded by eager native beauties, an agonized scream is heard offscreen. "That's Errol Flynn," Hope explains. "He can't stand it."

Lamour asks the two men if they always fight over women. "Why not? We never had any money," Bing says.

Hope stares at the camera and explains for his fellow millionaire: "That's for Washington."

When Crosby starts to croon a love lyric to Lamour, Hope tells the audience: "He's going to sing, folks. Now's the time to go out and get popcorn."

144

The Farces

What is farce?

Critics and lexicographers have agonized over the question for centuries, and none has provided a satisfying definition. The Random House Dictionary of the English Language offers as good an explanation as any: "a light, humorous play in which plot depends upon a skillfully exploited situation, rather than upon the development of character."

However it can be defined, farce is indisputably the most hazardous of comedy forms, requiring a touch that is sure, yet transparent. Without the proper ingredients and the finesse of master chefs, the soufflé becomes a pancake.

No comedian of the sound era can play farce with greater surety than Bob Hope. His deftness with lines, no matter how outrageous, makes him an ideal farceur.

Nothing but the Truth (1941) demonstrates how comfortably Hope fits into a farcical situation. It is strictly a one-joke script: how a man can exist for twenty-four hours without telling a falsehood, no matter how trivial. Hope enters into such a bet for $10,000 with Edward Arnold, Leif Erikson, and Glenn Anders. Astonishingly, the single joke works throughout, not only lending credence to the farcical proceedings, but also affording a tantalizing cliff-hanger. It is an amusing commentary on human nature and the incapacity of even the most honest of individuals to tell the truth.

Hope's character as stockbroker Steve Bennett is without any comic accouterments. He is something of a bumbler, and more gullible than most, but otherwise he plays it straight. The intriguing side of his character emerges when he begins the truth-telling bet. One shares his agonizing thought processes as he weighs the consequences of blurting out what he really believes to be true.

Caught in the Draft
(with Dorothy Lamour
and Clarence Kolb)

Elliott Nugent sustains the suspense throughout the film, and there is a real sense of relief when the bet is over and Hope can return to lying.

The majority of the Hope films in his early period were farces. Many were topical in nature and need to be considered in their historical context. *Caught in the Draft* (1941) touches on the prewar draft Army with amusing results. Hope is cast as Don Bolton, a self-devoted movie star who plays a convincing hero in a war scene but admits, "I even jump when someone cracks his knuckles."

Hope tries jumping off a piano to flatten his feet, but he gets drafted anyway. He arrives at the army camp with golf clubs and tennis racket, and he receives all the letters at mail call. Reacting to his antics are two of the best of the apoplectic actors—Paul Hurst as the sergeant, and Clarence Kolb as camp commander.

Hope is aided by second bananas Eddie Bracken and Lynne Overman and by a succession of topical gags. While cleaning fish on KP, Hope finds a Willkie button. After one of Hope's misdeeds, Kolb threatens, "If he gets in one more jam, he'll be in the guardhouse so long, Roosevelt will be out ahead of him!" Hope answers, "For life, huh?"

Let's Face It (1943) places Hope in the wartime Army, and this time the jokes are about meat and gasoline rationing and rubber shortages. The farce has complications that would give pause even to the French. There are five threesomes: three philandering businessmen; their suspicious wives; three soldiers the wives hire to make their husbands jealous; the soldiers' three girl friends; three floozies the husbands bring to a resort residence.

Somehow Sidney Lanfield manages to converge all fifteen in the final reel and maintain a degree of credibility.

The finale is funny if extraneous: Hope in a rowboat captures an enemy submarine by holding a mirror to the periscope, sending the sub aground.

The third military farce was postwar: *Off Limits* (1953). This time Hope is a prizefight manager forced by mobsters to join the Army and protect their champion, Stanley Clements. Then Clements is rejected, and Hope is forced to fulfill his enlistment. His efforts to feign insanity provide laughs, as do his encounters with the regulation-quoting sergeant, the offbeat comic Eddie Mayehoff. Mickey Rooney, as the championship prospect, proves an excellent foil for Hope.

146

Two musical farces offer a degree of entertainment, but fail to achieve their potential.

In *Louisiana Purchase* (1941), Hope plays the role created by William Gaxton in the Broadway show, which satirized the political corruption in the state of Louisiana. Paramount's concern about offending Louisianans is shown in a prologue sung by a studio lawyer. He advises the producers to make the state fictional, and a gaggle of chorus girls sings a number about "a mythical state called Louisiana."

Hope portrays the figurehead for a syndicate of crooked politicians, but it is never clear whether he is an unwitting victim of their chicanery. Victor Moore plays an investigating senator, a repeat of his Broadway role. When he remarks that he wants to see the syndicate's books, Hope replies, "Didn't you hear about the fire we're having—er, had?"

The musical numbers are handled by Zorina and the comedy by Moore. Hope's one big scene comes when he launches into a filibuster in the Louisiana legislature. The similarity to *Mr. Smith Goes to Washington* is not overlooked.

"You can't do this!" Moore protests.

"Oh yes, I can," Hope insists. "I got special permission from Jimmy Stewart."

Louisiana Purchase
(with Victor Moore)

Here Come the Girls (1953) offers a promising situation for farce: Hope as "the world's oldest living chorus boy," living with his doting mother and an exasperated stepfather. Again the mistaken identity theme, with Hope made star of a Broadway show so he can play decoy for a murderous Jack the Slasher.

The clumsy chorus boy makes a wreckage of the show, yet he can perform a challenge dance with the Step Brothers with great ease. That's just one of the ambiguities of a script that moves from slapstick to menace. Still, Hope has some funny rountines, and the musical numbers have the lavish look of Hollywood in the 1950s.

The titles of *Fancy Pants* (1950) list him as "Mr. Robert Hope (formerly Bob)" and he appears on the screen with monocle and sneer to announce: "No popcorn during my performance, peasants." That heralds his role as a gentleman's gentleman in a farcical fourth version of *Ruggles of Red Gap* (played by Taylor Holmes in 1918, Edward Everett Horton in 1923, and Charles Laughton in 1935). The casting seems ideal, but there is some uncertainty about Hope's role. Instead of an English butler, he seems to be an American actor playing an English butler in a London play.

The vehicle provides some good slapstick in the George Marshall tradition, with Hope spilling a tea tray in a dowager's lap. He remains cool: "Shall I draw the blinds? Shall I draw your bath? Draw your picture?"

The Great Lover (1949) places Hope in another outrageous situation: as a newspaperman who leads a boys' club through a European tour. Nearly all the action takes place on an ocean liner, with Hope involved with a card sharp and murderer (Roland Young), a penniless nobleman (Roland Culver), and his beautiful daughter (Rhonda Fleming). It is one of Hope's more pleasant comedies, with enough slapstick to keep things lively.

Jack Benny does an amusing walk-on in *The Great Lover*, playing a passenger who cashes a $100 bill for Hope. When Benny examines the bill with a jeweler's glass, Hope remarks, "I don't want to hock it; I just want to change it." As Benny strolls away, Hope thinks he recognizes him, then shrugs, "No, *he* wouldn't be traveling first class."

Here Come the Girls
(with the Step Brothers)

Fancy Pants (with Lea Penman)

149

The Comedies of Character

Sorrowful Jones
(with Lucille Ball)

The careers of most film comedians eventually ended because the public became too well acquainted with the nuances of the single characters they played on the screen. Overexposure is dangerous to all but the most durable of film stars. For comics it can be fatal, for they are deprived of that element which is essential to all comedy—surprise.

Bob Hope's career could have waned if he had continued playing the character audiences enjoyed in his first twenty films and on his radio show. The first indication that he could sublimate his highly successful comedic personality in a role of different dimensions came with *Sorrowful Jones* (1949).

The role was out of Damon Runyon's sideshow of Broadway denizens, and it had been played straight by Adolphe Menjou in *Little Miss Marker*. The remake, written by Hope veterans Mel Shavelson, Edmund Hartmann, and Jack Rose, stressed the comedic rather than the tearjerker aspects of the tale, but serious elements remained.

The character of the smalltime bookie is described by narrator Walter Winchell: "This is Sorrowful Jones, who fell in love with money at the age of six, and they've been going steady ever since." Sorrowful is introduced on a stroll down Broadway—fighting with a newsboy over a dropped coin, trying to lift a pencil from a blind peddler, making note of a horse bet by an undertaker, stopping at a barbershop to trim his ragged collar. He also runs into an old girl friend, Gladys O'Neil (Lucille Ball), who says, "It's been four years since I saw you, Sorrowful, but I recognize the suit."

The Hope wisecracks remain, but he slips into the new character with ease. He wears a hat at all times, the necktie is askew, and there is a cynical edge to the voice. His scorn is eloquent for

151

The Lemon Drop Kid

those horseplayers who seek to lay bets on credit. Nor is he softened by the enforced custody of the small girl—her father leaves her in the bookie parlor as a "marker" for his bet, then is murdered by Bruce Cabot's thugs. When the girl insists on being sung to sleep, he tries "Sweet Adeline," finally reads her to sleep from the *Daily Racing Form.*

The difference between a round and flat character, said E. M. Forster, is the ability to surprise. Hope's Sorrowful manages that. He transforms from the flinthearted cynic and defies the mob for the sake of Martha Jane. The ending is slapstick—Hope brings the girl's pet racehorse to her hospital room—but the moment of her recovery is played for sentiment. It is, in fact, the first sentimental scene in a Hope movie.

The Lemon Drop Kid (1951) offers the same combination— Hope, Runyon, Sidney Lanfield as director—without the same sure touch.

This time Hope is a racetrack tout and a notorious loser. Leaving Florida after being threatened by mobster Fred Clark, Hope arrives in a New York blizzard wearing a white suit. There is a funny scene in which he shaves, applies powder and lotion to his face, and brushes his teeth, bringing all the necessary articles from the pockets of his suit. As an afterthought, he sprinkles some powder on the suit to whiten it. It is a splendid characterization of a man accustomed to being on the lam, yet earnestly seeking to maintain appearances.

The Lemon Drop Kid has a variety of comedy gimmicks, including an outrageous sequence with Hope masquerading as an old lady. (One of the guests at the old ladies' home stares at the jumble of yarn and asks what he is knitting. "A mop," he answers.) What the film lacks is the purity of the Runyon form, with its juxtaposition of cynicism and sentiment.

The Seven Little Foys (1955) is the best of the Comedies of Character, and one of Hope's most satisfying films.

Here he attempts a biographical concept for the first time, and there is no compromise. The natural Hope exuberance is never visible. Instead, he becomes the case-hardened Irish-American vaudevillian Eddie Foy, who proclaims: "I'm not interested in dogs, women, or children—in the order of their importance."

He plays a defiant Foy, tilting his cigar at a hostile world. Even when he falls for a pretty Italian ballerina (Milly Vitale), he proposes marriage as though he had been trapped into it by an unfriendly fate. Then he virtually abandons her and their

That Certain Feeling

mushrooming family. Only when his wife dies does he realize his
neglect. After he learns the news, he checks the children's beds.
Young Bryan wakens and says, "Hello, Pop—just passing
through?"

The Seven Little Foys

Hope plays the tragedy with conviction. But the character of
Foy is not transformed. He stays at home with the kids, but de-
votes his attention to his cigars, whiskey, and racing form. Finally
he decides to put the children to work, and the conversion into
the family act provides some amusing sequences.

The Seven Little Foys ranks with *Yankee Doodle Dandy* and
the best of the show-biz biographies. Indeed, the most electric
moment comes when James Cagney repeats his George M. Cohan
characterization and performs a challenge dance with Foy at a
Friars Club banquet.

That Certain Feeling (1956) continues Hope's conversion from
comic to comedy actor. An adaptation of the Jean Kerr-Eleanor
Brooke play, *The King of Hearts,* the film casts Hope as Francis
X. Digman, a gifted but luckless cartoonist. His former wife, Eva
Marie Saint, gets him a job as ghost for her fiancé, a successful
cartoonist, George Sanders.

The Hope character is well-drawn. He has been defeated by

153

career and marriage failure, and he allows himself to be demeaned by the snobbish, overbearing Sanders. Whenever Hope tries to take a stand, he is defeated by a queasy stomach, for which he is consulting a psychiatrist. He has a charmingly offhanded way of brushing aside compliments; "Comes and goes," he mutters.

That Certain Feeling is perhaps Bob Hope's most sophisticated film, but it affords an ending of pure slapstick: a fouled-up visit to Sanders' apartment by the Edward R. Murrow television show, "Person to Person."

Beau James (1957) provides Hope's second biography, and his most difficult assignment. James Walker, the fun-loving mayor of New York City during Prohibition times, was a colorful figure but hardly a sympathetic one; an adulterer in his private life, his political career was ended by accusations of corruption. Script writers Jack Rose and Mel Shavelson couldn't quite reconcile these contradictory elements to film entertainment, which was what *Beau James* attempted to be.

Yet it is an interesting film, and it affords Hope one of his most complex characterizations. He plays most of the film straight; when he wisecracks, it is in the Walker manner. Since Walker was a song writer and a sometime entertainer, musical numbers fit into the film with logic. There is a delightful sequence in which Hope

Bachelor in Paradise
(with Robert Sterling)

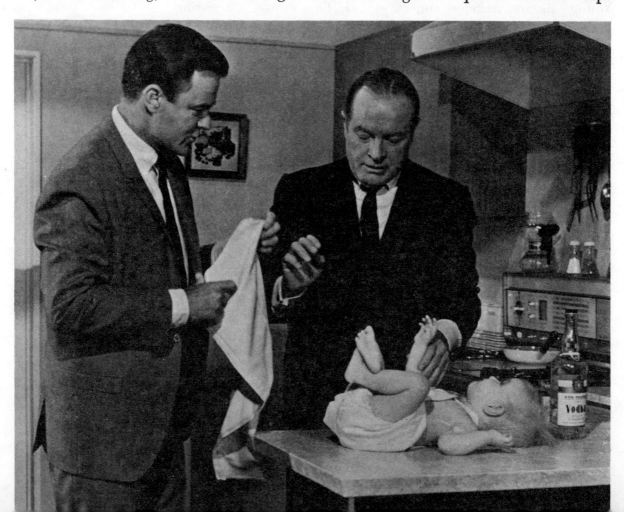

sings Walker's hit song, "Will You Love Me in December As You Do in May?" before ethnic groups. He delivers the lyrics in Italian and Yiddish, does a tap dance with a Negro girl in Harlem. Then at a campaign dinner he finds himself unbriefed on what nationality he is addressing. In his speech he mentions Garibaldi, Lafayette, Bolívar, and other ethnic heroes without a response. Desperate, he recites a series of countries until finally Latvia draws an enormous cheer.

Beau James is essentially a tragedy, the only one that Hope has played. Because of his personal and political foibles, Walker's career goes downhill. He is forced to plead for his political life before Franklin D. Roosevelt, governor of New York: "No matter whether misunderstood or not, I did my best."

His best isn't good enough, and he announces his intention to quit after he is booed at Yankee Stadium. "I wasn't the only chump in this city," he tells the crowd. "It took a lot of you to elect me."

Perhaps because of its tragic nature, *Beau James* did not enjoy the same success as *The Seven Little Foys*. But it remains interesting for its view of Hope at his most dramatic—and succeeding at it.

Bachelor in Paradise (1961) presents Hope in another character part, but without any dramatic pretensions. This time he is an author of best sellers about the intimate habits of peoples in foreign lands. Because his business manager has absconded with his funds, Hope is forced to return to the United States. His publisher, John McGiver, assigns Hope to live in a California housing tract to research a book on the habits of American suburbia.

The rest is a lighthearted concoction that combines wry commentary on suburbia with romantic farce. In one sequence Hope overloads the washer with detergent and fills his house with suds. The fire department is summoned.

Fireman: Where's the fire?

Hope: No fire.

Fireman: Then why did you call the fire department?

Hope: If I hollered "Soap!" who'd come?

In *A Global Affair* (1964), Hope plays a department head in the Human Rights section of the United Nations. The character is obviously straight, but not well defined. The comedy derives from Hope's dealings with women of all nations and with the foundling placed in his care (he diapers the child with the aid of powdered sugar and Scotch tape).

Beau James

155

The Domestic Comedies

The films that Hope has done in the latter period of his career have generally cast him as husband and/or father, beset with the troubles that seem unique to families in the mid-twentieth century. The most contemporary of the films was *How to Commit Marriage* (1971), which dealt amusingly with the ever widening generation gap. The casting was especially fortunate: Jane Wyman as Hope's divorcing wife; Jackie Gleason as Jackie Gleason.

The best of the domestic comedies was *The Facts of Life* (1960), a happy renewal of the association of Hope and Lucille Ball, and a reunion with the blithe talents of Mel Frank and Norman Panama; they co-authored the script and Frank directed.

As Mr. Hope elucidated earlier in this volume, *The Facts of Life* presented a challenge to the film makers. Audiences everywhere were so familiar with the on-camera characteristics of Hope and Ball that it remained a question whether Panama and Frank could establish the pair as living, breathing characters in a feature-length comedy.

Hope is presented as a glib comic—but the amateur kind, tossing lame jokes for the golf awards dinner at the suburban country club. Ball is the housewife and mother of two—but she is bored with her life and disgruntled with the gambling habits of her husband, Don DeFore. She yawns at Hope's jokes, and he says bitterly, "Would you like to leave a call?"

The two couples go home after the country club dinner, Hope with his wife, Ruth Hussey, who floats in her own world of children and household affairs. They are all embarking on a ritual vacation with another couple, and Ball laments the prospect of "six days of old Laughing Boy's enforced cheerfulness." Nor is Hope relishing the vacation with "Milton Berle in bloomers."

Neither of their spouses can leave, and Hope and Ball find themselves thrown together on the plane to Acapulco. They talk in two-word sentences until she learns that he is a weekend painter. They warm to each other and she suggests: "Let's make a pact: no jokes. You don't tell 'em and I don't have to laugh at 'em."

The romance starts when they go marlin fishing together and in a touching scene discover that they attended the same high school. Their affection for each other grows, and the rest of the comedy concerns what they are going to do about it. At first, both agree reluctantly that any kind of liaison would be senseless. Later, they're unable to resist.

The film's most hilarious sequence comes when they attempt a motel idyl, only to have Hope lose track of where he had left her. Later they go off for a weekend of passion in a mountain cabin. But they are plagued by a rainstorm, a balky convertible top, a leaky cabin, and their own nagging consciences. Then it's a race to get back home in time to intercept the "Dear John" note Ball had left for her husband.

Aside from its effectiveness as a domestic comedy, *The Facts of Life* offers profound insight on the vapidity of middle-class American living. Its treatment of incipient adultery was remarkably daring at a time when the censor's blue pencil still marked up movie scripts. One wonders how *The Facts of Life* might be filmed today.

The Facts of Life
(with Lucille Ball)

THE FILMS OF BOB HOPE

Casts, Credits, and Synopses

SHORT COMEDIES OF BOB HOPE

GOING SPANISH
Educational Films, 1934.

CAST

Bob Hope, Leah Ray.

CREDITS

Directed by Al Christie. Screenplay by William Watson and Art Jarrett.

PAREE, PAREE
Warner Brothers, 1934.

CAST

Bob Hope, Dorothy Stone, Charles Collins, Billie Leonard, Lorraine Collier.

CREDITS

Directed by Roy Mack. From the musical Fifty Million Frenchmen *by Herbert Fields, E. Ray Goetz, and Cole Porter. Screenplay by Crus Wood.*

THE OLD GREY MAYOR
Warner Brothers, 1935.

CAST

Bob Hope, Ruth Blasco, Lionel Stander, Sam Wren, George Watts.

CREDITS

Directed by Lloyd French. Screenplay by Dolph Singer and Jack Henley.

WATCH THE BIRDIE
Warner Brothers, 1935.

CAST

Bob Hope, Neil O'Day, Arline Dinitz, George Watts, Marie Nordstrom.

CREDITS

Directed by Lloyd French. Screenplay by Dolph Singer and Jack Henley.

DOUBLE EXPOSURE
Warner Brothers, 1935.

CAST

Bob Hope, Jules Epailley, Johnny Berkes, Lorretta Sayers.

CREDITS

Directed by Lloyd French. Screenplay by Jack Henley and Burnett Hershey.

CALLING ALL TARS
Warner Brothers, 1936.

CAST

Bob Hope, Johnny Berkes, Oscar Ragland.

CREDITS

Directed by Lloyd French. Screenplay by Jack Henley and Burnett Hershey.

SHOP TALK
Warner Brothers, 1936.

CAST

Bob Hope.

CREDITS

Directed by Lloyd French. Screenplay by Jack Henley and Burnett Hershey.

Hope has also appeared as himself in such shorts as: *Don't Hook Now*, Paramount, 1938, about the Bing Crosby golf tournament; *Welcome to Britain*, 1943, a film instructing American soldiers how to behave in England; *All-Star Bond Rally*, 20th Century-Fox, 1945, and *Hollywood Victory Caravan*, Paramount, 1945, concerning wartime bond selling; *The Heart of Show Business*, Columbia, 1957, about the Variety Clubs; and *Hollywood Star-Spangled Revue*, Warner Brothers, 1966, promoting U. S. Treasury bonds.

FEATURE FILMS

THE BIG BROADCAST OF 1938

Paramount. Released February 18, 1938.

CAST

W. C. Fields, Martha Raye, Dorothy Lamour, Shirley Ross, Lynne Overman, Bob Hope, Ben Blue, Leif Erikson, Grace Bradley, Rufe Davis, Patricia Wilder, Lionel Pape, Dorothy Howe, Russell Hicks, Kirsten Flagstad, Tito Guizar, Shep Fields and His Orchestra, Wilfred Pelletier.

CREDITS

Produced by Harlan Thompson. Directed by Mitchell Leisen. Story by Frederick Hazlitt Brennan. Screenplay by Walter De Leon, Francis Martin, Ken Englund. Adaptation by Howard Lindsay and Russel Crouse. Photographed by Harry Fishbeck. Musical Direction by Boris Morros. Dance Direction by LeRoy Prinz. Special Effects by Gordon Jennings. Edited by Eda Warren, Chandler House. Running time, 90 minutes.

SYNOPSIS

Two ocean liners engage in a transatlantic race. One is owned by T. Frothingwell Bellows (*W. C. Fields*), who has a wild daughter, Martha (*Martha Raye*). Buzz Fielding (*Bob Hope*) is a radio announcer with three ex-wives seeking alimony. *Variety* once offered $10,000 to anyone who could tell the film's plot. So far no one has collected. Hope and Shirley Ross sing "Thanks for the Memory," which won the Academy Award for best song. Other songs include: "You Took the Words Right Out of My Heart," "Mama, the Moon Is Here Again," and "The Waltz Lives On."

Hope and Shirley Ross

Paramount.   Released April 29, 1938.

CAST

George Burns, Gracie Allen, Martha Raye, Bob Hope, Edward Everett Horton, Florence George, Ben Blue, Betty Grable, Jackie Coogan, John Payne, Cecil Cunningham, Robert Cummings, Skinnay Ennis, Slate Brothers, Jerry Colonna, Charles Colonna, Charles Trowbridge, Jerry Bergen, Tully Marshall, Edward LeSaint.

CREDITS

Produced by Lewis Gensler. Directed by Raoul Walsh. Story by Frederick Hazlitt Brennan from idea of Ted Lesser. Screenplay by Walter De Leon, Francis Martin. Photographed by Victor Milner. Edited by LeRoy Stone. Running time, 86 minutes.

FRONT ROW: Skinnay Ennis, John Payne, Florence George, Hope, Martha Raye, Jackie Coogan, Betty Grable, George Burns, Gracie Allen, Edward Everett Horton, Cecil Cunningham, Ben Blue; BEHIND, the Slate Brothers

SYNOPSIS

Gracie Alden (*Gracie Allen*) inherits a small-town college and turns it into bedlam. She reorganizes the school and imports vaudeville actors to conduct the classes. A faint plot on which to hang a succession of musical and comedy numbers. Hope plays Bud Brady, a brash manager. Songs include: "What a Rumba Does to Romance," "How'dja Like to Love Me?" and "I Fall in Love with You Every Day."

COLLEGE SWING

GIVE ME A SAILOR

Nana Bryant, Betty Grable, Martha Raye, Jack Whiting, Hope

Paramount.   Released Aug. 19, 1938.

CAST

Martha Raye, Bob Hope, Betty Grable, Jack Whiting, Clarence Kolb, J. C. Nugent, Bonnie Jean Churchill, Nana Bryant.

CREDITS

Produced by Jeff Lazarus. Associate Producer, Paul Jones. Directed by Elliott Nugent. From a play by Anne Nichols. Screenplay by Doris Anderson, Frank Butler. Dance Direction by LeRoy Prinz. Musical Direction by Boris Morros. Photographed by Victor Milner. Edited by William Shea. Running time, 80 minutes.

SYNOPSIS

Two Navy officers (*Bob Hope* and *Jack Whiting*) are in love with Nancy Larkin (*Betty Grable*). Nancy's plain sister, Letty (*Martha Raye*), conspires with Bob to sabotage Jack's romance. No luck. Then Letty wins a contest for the most beautiful legs, and Jack transfers his affection to her. But Letty dashes out in a Navy Day parade to hunt for Bob. Lots of slapstick en route. Songs include "What Goes On Here in My Heart?" and "A Little Kiss at Twilight."

Paramount.   Released Nov. 11, 1938.

CAST

Bob Hope, Shirley Ross, Charles Butterworth, Otto Kruger, Hedda Hopper, Patricia Wilder, Roscoe Karns, Laura Hope Crews, William Collier, Sr., Emma Dunn, Edward Gargan, Eddie Anderson, Jack Norton.

CREDITS

Associate Producer, Mel Shauer. Directed by George Archainbaud. From a play by Albert Hackett, Frances Goodrich. Screenplay by Lynn Starling. Musical Direction by Boris Morros. Photographed by Karl Struss. Edited by Alma Ruth Macrorie. Running time, 77 minutes.

SYNOPSIS

Newlyweds Steve (*Bob Hope*) and Anne Merrick (*Shirley Ross*) agree that she should go back to work as a model to support his ambitions to be an author. They run into disagreements and their separation inspires him to finish his book. The title song is reprised, and the married couple also sings "Two Sleepy People."

THANKS FOR THE MEMORY

Shirley Ross and Hope

NEVER SAY DIE

Paramount.   Released April 14, 1939.

CAST

Martha Raye, Bob Hope, Andy Devine, Alan Mowbray, Gale Sondergaard, Sig Rumann, Ernest Cossart, Paul Harvey, Frances Arms, Ivan Simpson, Monty Woolley, Foy Van Dolsen, Christian Rub.

CREDITS

Produced by Paul Jones. Directed by Elliott Nugent. From a play by William H. Post. Screenplay by Don Hartman, Frank Butler, Preston Sturges. Musical Direction by Boris Morros. Photographed by Leo Tover. Special Effects by Farciot Edouart. Edited by James Smith. Running time, 80 minutes.

SYNOPSIS

John Kidley (*Bob Hope*) is a multi-millionaire eccentric who is given a month to live when a chemist switches his analysis with a dog's. Kidley escapes marriage with an adventuress, Juno (*Gale Sondergaard*), and meets Mickey Hawkins (*Martha Raye*), daughter of a Texas oilman who wants her to marry a prince (*Alan Mowbray*) instead of her sweetheart (*Andy Devine*). Kidley marries Mickey so she can inherit his fortune and marry her real beau. Then he discovers he's not doomed to die, and he's in love with Mickey. Adapted from a William H. Post play filmed as a silent in 1924. Among the Rainger-Robin songs: "The Tra La La and the Oom Pah Pah."

Hope, Christian Rub, and Martha Raye

SOME LIKE IT HOT

Paramount.   Released May 19, 1939.

CAST

Bob Hope, Shirley Ross, Una Merkel, Gene Krupa, Rufe Davis, Bernard Nedell, Frank Sully, Bernadene Hayes, Richard Denning, Clarence H. Wilson, Dudley Dickerson, Harry Barris, Wayne (Tiny) Whitt, Edgar Dearing, Jack Smart.

CREDITS

Associate Producer, William C. Thomas. Directed by George Archainbaud. From a play by Ben Hecht, Gene Fowler. Screenplay by Lewis R. Foster, Wilkie C. Mahoney. Music Advisor, Arthur Franklin. Photographed by Karl Struss. Edited by Edward Dmytryk. Running time, 64 minutes.

SYNOPSIS

Nicky Nelson (*Bob Hope*) is a fast-talking barker for a board-walk amusement parlor. He hires Gene Krupa and a small band to ballyhoo his buried-alive show. He aims to book Krupa in the dance hall operated by Stephen Hanratty (*Bernard Nedell*), but loses the booking—and his enterprise. He also loses his sweetheart, Lily Racquel (*Shirley Ross*), but all ends well. Songs: "The Lady's in Love with You," "Some Like It Hot." No relation to the 1959 film of the same title, starring Marilyn Monroe. Because of the title confusion, the Hope version plays on television under the title *Rhythm Romance*.

Front Row of Bandstand: Gene Krupa (LEFT), Hope, Rufe Davis, Harry Barris (RIGHT)

THE CAT AND THE CANARY

Paramount.   Released Nov. 10, 1939.

CAST

Bob Hope, Paulette Goddard, John Beal, Douglass Montgomery, Gale Sondergaard, Elizabeth Patterson, Nydia Westman,
George Zucco, John Wray, George Regas.

CREDITS

*Produced by Arthur Hornblow, Jr. Directed by Elliott Nugent.
From a play by John Willard. Screenplay by Walter De Leon,
Lynn Starling. Musical Score by Dr. Ernst Toch. Musical Advisor,
Andrea Setaro. Photographed by Charles Lang. Edited by Archie
Marshek. Running time, 72 minutes.*

SYNOPSIS

Prospective heirs to a fortune are assembled at the bayou home
of an eccentric millionaire ten years after his death. The will is
read, and the fortune has been left to Joyce Norman (*Paulette
Goddard*). Spooky things begin to happen, and three murders
occur. Although thoroughly frightened, Wallie Campbell (*Bob
Hope*) solves the murders and wins the girl. A remake of a 1927
Universal silent film of the same title, based on the old Broadway
thriller by John Willard.

Gale Sondergaard, Paulette Goddard, Hope, George Zucco

ROAD TO SINGAPORE

Paramount.   Released March 22, 1940.

CAST

Bing Crosby, Dorothy Lamour, Bob Hope, Charles Coburn, Judith Barrett, Anthony Quinn, Jerry Colonna, Johnny Arthur, Pierre Watkin, Gaylord Pendleton, Miles Mander, Pedro Regas, Greta Granstedt, John Kelly, Ed Gargan, Kitty Kelly, Roger Gray, Benny Inocencio, Gloria Franklin, Carmen D'Antonio, Paula de Cardo.

CREDITS

Produced by Harlan Thompson. Directed by Victor Schertzinger. Story by Harry Hervey. Screenplay by Don Hartman, Frank Butler. Dance Direction by LeRoy Prinz. Musical Direction by Victor Young. Photographed by William C. Mellor. Edited by Paul Weatherwax. Running time, 84 minutes.

SYNOPSIS

Josh Mallon (*Bing Crosby*) and Ace Lannigan (*Bob Hope*) escape to the South Seas to avoid the toils of two women aiming at matrimony. They land on the exotic island of Kaigoon, where they encounter the beautiful Mima (*Dorothy Lamour*) as well as the infamous Caesar (*Anthony Quinn*). Songs: "Too Romantic," "Sweet Potato Piper," "Kaigoon," "The Moon and the Willow Tree."

Dorothy Lamour, Bing Crosby, and Hope

THE GHOST BREAKERS

Paramount.   Released June 21, 1940.

CAST

Bob Hope, Paulette Goddard, Richard Carlson, Paul Lukas, Anthony Quinn, Willie Best, Pedro de Cordoba, Virginia Brissac, Noble Johnson, Tom Dugan, Paul Fix, Lloyd Corrigan.

CREDITS

Produced by Arthur Hornblow, Jr. Directed by George Marshall. From a play by Paul Dickey, Charles Goddard. Screenplay by Walter De Leon. Photographed by Charles Lang. Edited by Ellsworth Hoagland. Running time, 82 minutes.

SYNOPSIS

Larry Lawrence (*Bob Hope*) is a radio commentator who innocently becomes involved in a murder. Mary Carter (*Paulette Goddard*) saves him from the police and he escapes in a trunk on a Cuba-bound steamer. They become romantically involved, and he offers to help her rid her spooky island and castle of ghosts.

Paulette Goddard, Paul Lukas, and Hope

ROAD TO ZANZIBAR

Paramount. Released April 11, 1941.

CAST

Bing Crosby, Bob Hope, Dorothy Lamour, Una Merkel, Eric Blore, Luis Alberni, Joan Marsh, Ethel Greer, Iris Adrian, Georges Renavent.

CREDITS

Produced by Paul Jones. Directed by Victor Schertzinger. Story by Don Hartman, Sy Bartlett. Screenplay by Frank Butler, Don Hartman. Photographed by Ted Tetzlaff. Edited by Alma Macrorie. Running time, 92 minutes.

SYNOPSIS

Chuck Reardon (*Bing Crosby*) and Fearless Frazier (*Bob Hope*) are American sideshow artists in darkest Africa. Chuck is always figuring out some wild money-making scheme while Fearless wants only to get back home. Two stranded girls (*Dorothy Lamour, Una Merkel*) persuade the boys to take them on a long safari. They run into cannibals, wild beasts, and other hazards. Songs: "It's Always You," "You're Dangerous," "You Lucky People, You," "African Etude," title theme.

Bing Crosby, Hope, Una Merkel (IN BOX), and Dorothy Lamour

CAUGHT IN THE DRAFT

Andrew Tombes, Lynne Overman, Hope, Dorothy Lamour, Eddie Bracken

Paramount. Released July 4, 1941.

CAST

Bob Hope, Dorothy Lamour, Lynne Overman, Eddie Bracken, Clarence Kolb, Paul Hurst, Ferike Boros, Phyllis Ruth, Irving Bacon, Arthur Loft, Edgar Dearing.

CREDITS

Produced by B. G. DeSylva. Directed by David Butler. Story and Screenplay by Harry Tugend. Additional Dialogue by Wilkie C. Mahoney. Musical Score by Victor Young. Photographed by Karl Struss. Edited by Irene Morra. Running time, 82 minutes.

SYNOPSIS

Movie star Don Bolton (*Bob Hope*) enlists in the Army to win the hand of Tony Fairbanks (*Dorothy Lamour*), daughter of the Colonel (*Clarence Kolb*). His agent (*Lynne Overman*) and chauffeur (*Eddie Bracken*) enlist with him. The ex-actor proves the worst of soldiers, but he and his pals end up heroes.

Paramount.   Released Oct. 10, 1941.

CAST

Bob Hope, Paulette Goddard, Edward Arnold, Leif Erikson, Glenn Anders, Helen Vinson, Grant Mitchell, Willie Best, Clarence Kolb, Catherine Doucet, Mary Forbes, Rose Hobart, Leon Belasco, Helene Millard, William Wright, Oscar Smith, Dick Chandler, Catherine Craig, Edward McWade, Keith Richards, James Blaine, Jack Egan.

CREDITS

Produced by Arthur Hornblow, Jr. Directed by Elliott Nugent. From a play by James Montgomery and a novel by Frederic S. Isham. Screenplay by Don Hartman, Ken Englund. Photographed by Charles Lang. Edited by Alma Macrorie. Running time, 90 minutes.

SYNOPSIS

Steve Bennet (*Bob Hope*) makes a bet with three other stock-brokers (*Edward Arnold, Leif Erikson, Glenn Anders*) that he can tell the truth for twenty-four hours. His bet is $10,000, entrusted to him by Arnold's niece (*Paulette Goddard*). Complications arise when he attends a party aboard a lavish houseboat and is not allowed even the smallest white lie.

NOTHING BUT THE TRUTH

LOUISIANA PURCHASE

Paramount.   Released Dec. 25, 1941.

CAST

Bob Hope, Vera Zorina, Victor Moore, Irene Bordoni, Dona Drake, Raymond Walburn, Maxie Rosenbloom, Frank Albertson, Phyllis Ruth, Donald McBride, Andrew Tombes, Robert Warwick, Charles La Torre, Charles Lasky, Emory Parnell, Iris Meredith, Catherine Craig, Jack Norton, Sam McDaniels, Kay Aldridge, Katherine Booth, Alaine Brandes, Barbara Britton, Brooke Evans, Blanche Grady, Lynda Grey, Margaret Hayes, Louise La Planche, Barbara Slater, Eleanor Stewart, Jean Wallace.

CREDITS

Associate Producer, Harold Wilson. Directed by Irving Cummings. From the musical by Morrie Ryskind. Story by B. G. DeSylva. Screenplay by Jerome Chodorov, Joseph Fields. Photographed by Harry Hallenberger. Color Photography by Ray Rennahan. Edited by LeRoy Stone. Running time, 98 minutes.

SYNOPSIS

Jim Taylor (*Bob Hope*) is framed by his grafting associates of the Louisiana Purchasing Co. and he becomes the target of an investigation by U.S. senator Oliver P. Loganberry (*Victor Moore*). The grafters force Taylor to frame the senator, who is lured to the restaurant of Madame Bordelaise (*Irene Bordoni*). Taylor's girl friend (*Vera Zorina*) poses for a photograph on the senator's lap. All turns out well after Taylor conducts a filibuster on the legislature floor "through courtesy of Jimmy Stewart," who did it in *Mr. Smith Goes to Washington.* Irving Berlin songs include: "Louisiana Purchase," "You're Lonely and I'm Lonely," "It's a Lovely Day Tomorrow."

Hope, Irene Bordoni, and Victor Moore

MY FAVORITE BLONDE

Paramount.   Released March 18, 1942.

CAST

Bob Hope, Madeleine Carroll, Gale Sondergaard, George Zucco, Victor Varconi, Lionel Royce, Crane Whitley, Otto Reichow, Charles Cain, Walter Kingsford, Erville Alderson.

CREDITS

Associate Producer, Paul Jones. Directed by Sidney Lanfield. Story by Melvin Frank, Norman Panama. Screenplay by Don Hartman, Frank Butler. Photographed by William Mellor. Edited by William Shea. Running time, 78 minutes.

SYNOPSIS

Larry Haines (*Bob Hope*) is a smalltime variety show performer with a trained penguin. Karen Bentley (*Madeleine Carroll*) seeks his help in carrying secret instructions from the British government to the Lockheed factory in Los Angeles. Haines believes he is dealing with a beauteous but giddy blonde, but soon he is enmeshed with Nazi agents (*Gale Sondergaard* and *George Zucco*). The chase extends across the country. A brief appearance by Bing Crosby.

Hope, Madeleine Carroll, and body

Paramount. Released Oct. 5, 1942.

CAST

Bing Crosby, Bob Hope, Dorothy Lamour, Anthony Quinn, Dona Drake, Vladimir Sokoloff, Mikhail Rasumny, Jamiel Hanson, Monte Blue, Louise La Planche, Theo de Voe, Brooke Evans Suzanne Ridgeway, Patsy Mace, Yvonne De Carlo, Poppy Wilde, Ralph Penney, Dan Seymour.

CREDITS

Associate Producer, Paul Jones. Directed by David Butler. Screenplay by Frank Butler, Don Hartman. Musical Direction by Victor Young. Photographed by William Mellor. Edited by Irene Morra. Running time, 83 minutes.

SYNOPSIS

Jeff Peters (*Bing Crosby*) and Turkey Jackson (*Bob Hope*) land in Morocco after a shipwreck. Jeff sells Turkey into slavery to pay a dinner check, then tries to join him when Turkey becomes head man at the desert paradise of Princess Shalimar (*Dorothy Lamour*). The two adventurers run afoul of the sheik Mullay Kasim (*Anthony Quinn*) but manage to escape and sail for New York. Songs by Burke and Van Husen: "Moonlight Becomes You," "Constantly," "Ain't Got a Dime to My Name."

Dorothy Lamour, Bing Crosby, and Hope

ROAD TO MOROCCO

STAR SPANGLED RHYTHM

Hope on naval maneuvers

Paramount.   Released Dec. 31, 1942.

CAST

Bing Crosby, Ray Milland, Vera Zorina, Eddie Bracken, Bob Hope, Victor Moore, Mary Martin, Veronica Lake, Fred Mac-Murray, Dorothy Lamour, Dick Powell, Alan Ladd, Franchot Tone, Paulette Goddard, Betty Hutton, Rochester, William Bendix, Susan Hayward, Lynne Overman, Cass Daley, Walter Catlett, Jerry Colonna, Marjorie Reynolds, Gary Crosby, Ernest Truex, Sterling Holloway, Macdonald Carey, Betty Rhodes, Johnny Johnston, Katherine Dunham, Walter Abel, Dona Drake, Gil Lamb, Arthur Treacher, Cecil B. De Mille, Preston Sturges, Ralph Murphy, Anne Revere, Edward Fielding, Edgar Dearing, William Haade, Maynard Holmes, James Millican, Eddie Johnson, Slim and Slam, Walter Wahl, Golden Gate Quartette.

CREDITS

Associate producer, Joseph Sistrom. Directed by George Marshall. Screenplay by Harry Tugend. Musical Score by Robert Emmett Dolan. Photographed by Leo Tover. Edited by Arthur Schmidt. Running time, 99 minutes.

SYNOPSIS

A young sailor (*Eddie Bracken*) arrives in Hollywood to visit his father (*Victor Moore*), a studio gateman who has told his son he ran the studio. The studio switchboard operator (*Betty Hutton*) has been corresponding with the sailor and tries to maintain the deception. Everyone at the studio pitches in to carry on the charade. Bob Hope appears as master of ceremonies at a sailors' entertainment and takes part in skits. Songs by Johnny Mercer and Harold Arlen include "Old Glory," "That Old Black Magic," "Let's Hit the Road to Dreamland," and "I'm Doing It for Defense."

RKO Radio.   Released Jan. 4, 1943.

CAST

Bob Hope, Dorothy Lamour, Lenore Aubert, Otto Preminger, Eduardo Ciannelli, Marion Martin, Donald Meek, Phyllis Ruth, Philip Ahn, Donald McBride, Mary Treen, Bettye Avery, Margaret Hayes, Mary Byrne, William Tetter, Henry Guttman, Florence Bates, Walter Catlett, John Abbott, Frank Sully.

CREDITS

Produced by Samuel Goldwyn. Directed by David Butler. Story by Leonard Q. Ross, Leonard Spigelgass. Screenplay by Harry Kurnitz. Musical Score by Leigh Harline. Musical Direction by C. Bakaleinikoff. Photographed by Rudolph Mate. Special Effects by Ray Binger. Edited by Daniel Mandell. Running time, 95 minutes.

SYNOPSIS

Robert Kittredge (*Bob Hope*) is a foreign correspondent who is recalled from Moscow and discharged for having missed the story of the German invasion of Russia. He tries to regain his job by exposing Axis saboteurs. A Romanian fugitive (*John Abbott*) gives him the story. Kittredge and his fiancée, Christina Hill (*Dorothy Lamour*), become entangled with a spy ring. After many mishaps he captures the spies singlehandedly.

THEY GOT ME COVERED

Eduardo Ciannelli and Hope

LET'S FACE IT

Betty Hutton and Hope

Paramount. Released Aug. 5, 1943.

CAST

Bob Hope, Betty Hutton, Zasu Pitts, Phyllis Povah, Dave Willock, Eve Arden, Cully Richards, Marjorie Weaver, Dona Drake, Raymond Walburn, Andrew Tombes, Arthur Loft, Joe Sawyer, Grace Hayle, Evelyn Dockson, Andria Moreland, Kay Linaker, Brooke Evans.

CREDITS

Associate Producer, Fred Kohlmar. Directed by Sidney Lanfield. From the musical by Dorothy Fields, Herbert Fields, Cole Porter. Screenplay by Harry Tugend. Photographed by Lionel Lindon. Running time, 76 minutes.

SYNOPSIS

Jerry Walker (*Bob Hope*) and his soldier buddies Barney Hilliard (*Dave Willock*) and Frankie Burns (*Cully Richards*) are hired to act as gigolos. Three wives (*Eve Arden, Zasu Pitts, Phyllis Povah*) are seeking revenge on their philandering husbands. Complications arise when the soldiers' sweeties (*Betty Hutton, Dona Drake, Marjorie Weaver*) discover the reluctant love-making. Based on an old play, *Cradle Snatchers,* which was adapted as a Danny Kaye musical on Broadway. Songs include: "Who Did? I Did, Yes I Did," "Let's Face It," "Let's Not Talk About Love."

THE PRINCESS AND THE PIRATE

RKO Radio.   Released Oct. 17, 1944.

CAST

   Bob Hope, Virginia Mayo, Walter Brennan, Walter Slezak, Victor McLaglen, Marc Kuznetzoff, Brandon Hurst, Tom Kennedy, Stanley Andrews, Robert Warwick.

CREDITS

   Produced by Samuel Goldwyn. Associate Producer, Don Hartman. Directed by David Butler. Story by Sy Bartlett. Adaptation by Allen Boretz and Curtis Kenyon. Screenplay by Don Hartman, Melville Shavelson, Everett Freeman. Musical Score by David Rose. Photographed by Victor Milner. Special Effects by R. O. Binger, Clarence Slifer. Edited by Daniel Mandell. Running time, 94 minutes.

SYNOPSIS

   Sylvester the Great (*Bob Hope*) sails for America after a less than successful career as an actor in eighteenth-century England. Also on the boat is Princess Margaret (*Virginia Mayo*), who is fleeing incognito because her father won't allow her to marry a commoner. Their ship is sacked by pirates led by the Hook (*Victor McLaglen*). A half-witted buccaneer (*Walter Brennan*) helps the pair to escape to a pirate stronghold island and a raucous time ensues. Song: "Kiss Me in the Moonlight."

ROAD TO UTOPIA

Paramount.   Released Jan. 25, 1945.

CAST

Bing Crosby, Bob Hope, Dorothy Lamour, Hillary Brooke, Douglas Dumbrille, Jack La Rue, Robert Barrat, Nestor Paiva, Robert Benchley, Will Wright, Jimmy Dundee.

CREDITS

Produced by Paul Jones. Directed by Hal Walker. Screenplay by Norman Panama, Melvin Frank. Musical Score by Leigh Harline. Musical Direction by Robert Emmett Dolan. Dance Direction by Danny Dare. Animation by Jerry Fairbanks. Photographed by Lionel Lindon. Process Photography by Farciot Edouart. Edited by Stuart Gilmore. Running time, 90 minutes.

SYNOPSIS

Duke Johnson (*Bing Crosby*) and Chester Hooton (*Bob Hope*) are a couple of vaudevillians-con men who travel to Alaska in search of gold. They come across a stolen map that belongs to Sal (*Dorothy Lamour*). Murder, skulduggery, gunplay, and romance ensue. Songs: "Would You" and "Anybody's Dream."

Hope, Dorothy Lamour, and Bing Crosby

MONSIEUR BEAUCAIRE

Paramount.   Released Sept. 30, 1946.

CAST

Bob Hope, Joan Caulfield, Patric Knowles, Marjorie Reynolds, Cecil Kellaway, Joseph Schildkraut, Reginald Owen, Constance Collier, Hillary Brooke, Fortunio Bonanova, Mary Nash, Leonid Kinskey, Howard Freeman, Helen Freeman.

CREDITS

Produced by Paul Jones. Directed by George Marshall. From the novel by Booth Tarkington. Screenplay by Melvin Frank, Norman Panama. Musical Score by Robert Emmett Dolan. Photographed by James Brown. Edited by Richard Currier, Seth Larson. Running time, 93 minutes.

SYNOPSIS

Monsieur Beaucaire (*Bob Hope*) is barber to the French court and in love with the lovely scullery maid Mimi (*Joan Caulfield*). He gets in trouble with the king (*Reginald Owen*) and everyone else except the Duc de Chandre (*Patric Knowles*) who rescues him from the guillotine and takes him to the Spanish court. Beaucaire poses as a nobleman and gets in more trouble. Little resemblance to the Booth Tarkington book and virtually none to the 1924 film which starred Rudolph Valentino.

Joseph Schildkraut (LEFT) and Hope

Paramount.   Released April 4, 1947.

CAST

Bob Hope, Dorothy Lamour, Peter Lorre, Lon Chaney, John Hoyt, Charles Dingle, Reginald Denny, Frank Puglia, Ann Doran, Willard Robertson, Jack La Rue.

CREDITS

Produced by Daniel Dare. Directed by Elliott Nugent. Screenplay by Edmund Beloin, Jack Rose. Musical Score by Robert Emmett Dolan. Photographed by Lionel Lindon. Edited by Ellsworth Hoagland. Running time, 87 minutes.

SYNOPSIS

Ronnie Jackson (*Bob Hope*) asks permission to tell his story to the press before he goes to the gas chamber in San Quentin prison. He tells in flashback how he earned his living as a baby photographer though he yearned to be like the private detective next door. His ambitions entangle him with mystery woman Carlotta Montay (*Dorothy Lamour*) as well as a parade of sinister characters. He gets framed as murderer of a government official (*Reginald Denny*) but is exonerated at the last moment.

MY FAVORITE BRUNETTE

Bing Crosby and Hope with George Marshall

VARIETY GIRL

Paramount.   Released Aug. 29, 1947.

CAST

Mary Hatcher, Olga San Juan, De Forrest Kelley, William Demarest, Frank Faylen, Frank Ferguson, and Paramount contract players including Bob Hope.

CREDITS

Produced by Daniel Dare. Directed by George Marshall. Screenplay by Edmund Hartmann, Frank Tashlin, Robert Welch, Monte Brice. Musical Direction by Joseph J. Lilley, Troy Sanders. Photographed by Lionel Lindon, Stuart Thompson. Edited by LeRoy Stone. Running time, 83 minutes.

SYNOPSIS

Catherine Brown (*Mary Hatcher*) is the first foundling of the show business charity organization, Variety Clubs. She goes to Hollywood for a screen test. There she meets Amber LaVonne (*Olga San Juan*), who impersonates the girl to further her own career. Both girls come in contact with just about every star on the Paramount lot in 1947. Hope and Crosby appear in a song-and-dance number.

WHERE THERE'S LIFE

Hope, William Bendix, and Vera Marshe

Paramount.   Released Nov. 21, 1947.

CAST

Bob Hope, Signe Hasso, William Bendix, George Coulouris, Vera Marshe, George Zucco, Dennis Hoey, John Alexander, Victor Varconi, Joseph Vitale, Harry Von Zell.

CREDITS

Produced by Paul Jones. Directed by Sidney Lanfield. Story by Melville Shavelson. Screenplay by Allen Boretz, Melville Shavelson. Musical Direction by Irvin Talbot. Photographed by Charles B. Lang, Jr. Edited by Archie Marshek. Running time, 75 minutes.

SYNOPSIS

The king of a mythical kingdom confesses on his deathbed that he sired a son who now lives in America. He turns out to be Michael Valentine (*Bob Hope*), an all-night disc jockey for a dog food company. A delegation including a female army general (*Signe Hasso*) goes to New York to return him to his throne. Rival political factions aim to liquidate the new king; New York cop Victor O'Brien (*William Bendix*) gets involved in the rescue.

Paramount.   Released Dec. 25, 1947.

CAST

Bing Crosby, Bob Hope, Dorothy Lamour, Gale Sondergaard, Frank Faylen, Joseph Vitale, Frank Puglia, Nestor Paiva, Robert Barrat, Jerry Colonna, The Wiere Brothers, The Andrews Sisters.

CREDITS

Produced by Daniel Dare. Directed by Norman Z. McLeod. Screenplay by Edmund Beloin, Jack Rose. Musical Direction by Robert Emmett Dolan. Photographed by Ernest Laszlo. Edited by Ellsworth Hoagland. Running time, 100 minutes.

SYNOPSIS

Scat Sweeney (*Bing Crosby*) and Hot Lips Barton (*Bob Hope*) are a pair of broke musicians from Hollywood. They play a one-night stand at a carnival, burn the place down, then stow away on a liner for Rio de Janeiro. They encounter Lucia Maria de Andrade (*Dorothy Lamour*), whose sinister aunt (*Gale Sondergaard*) is marrying her off to a no-good. Sweeney and Barton discover the aunt is hypnotizing Lucia and the plot is broken up in a wild finale. Songs include : "But Beautiful," "You Don't Have to Know the Language," "Apalachicola, Fla.," "For What," "Experience."

THE ROAD TO RIO

THE PALEFACE

Paramount.   Released Dec. 24, 1948.

CAST

Bob Hope, Jane Russell, Robert Armstrong, Iris Adrian, Robert Watson, Jack Searl, Joseph Vitale, Charles Trowbridge, Clem Bevans, Jeff York, Stanley Andrews, Wade Crosby, Chief Yowlachie, Iron Eyes Cody.

CREDITS

Produced by Robert L. Welch. Directed by Norman Z. McLeod. Screenplay by Edmund Hartmann, Frank Tashlin. Musical Score by Victor Young. Photographed by Ray Rennahan. Edited by Ellsworth Hoagland. Running time, 91 minutes.

SYNOPSIS

Painless Potter (*Bob Hope*) is a correspondence-school dentist who takes his trade to the Wild West. He meets up with Calamity Jane (*Jane Russell*), who is seeking the culprit who is selling arms to the Indians; if she succeeds, she will be pardoned for earlier crimes. She marries the dentist to avoid suspicion, later falls for him. Potter becomes an unwilling hero when the culprits are captured. The song "Buttons and Bows," by Jay Livingston and Ray Evans, won the Academy Award for best film song of 1948.

SORROWFUL JONES

Paramount.   Released July 4, 1949.

CAST

Bob Hope, Lucille Ball, William Demarest, Bruce Cabot, Thomas Gomez, Tom Pedi, Paul Lees, Houseley Stevenson, Ben Weldon, Mary Jane Saunders.

CREDITS

Produced by Robert L. Welch. Directed by Sidney Lanfield. From the story by Damon Runyon. Screenplay by Melville Sha-velson, Edmund Hartmann, Jack Rose. Musical Score by Robert Emmett Dolan. Photographed by Daniel L. Fapp. Edited by Mary Kay Dodson. Running time, 88 minutes.

SYNOPSIS

Bookie Sorrowful Jones (*Bob Hope*) accepts a bet from a man who leaves his daughter Martha Jane (*Mary Jane Saunders*) as collateral. The bettor fails to return, and Sorrowful is forced to become a foster father. He learns the real father has been killed by gangsters over a racehorse fix. Night club singer Gladys O'Neil (*Lucille Ball*) helps Sorrowful take care of the little girl. Martha Jane is hurt in an accident and her recovery depends on seeing her beloved horse. She does. A remake of *Little Miss Marker*, which starred Shirley Temple in 1934.

Mary Jane Saunders, Hope, and Lucille Ball

THE GREAT LOVER

Paramount.   Released Dec. 28, 1949.

CAST

Bob Hope, Rhonda Fleming, Roland Young, Roland Culver, Richard Lyon, Gary Gray, Jerry Hunter, Jackie Jackson, Karl Wright Esser, Orley Lindgren, Curtis Loys Jackson, Jr., George Reeves, Jim Backus, Sig Arno.

CREDITS

Produced by Edmund Beloin. Directed by Alexander Hall. Screenplay by Edmund Beloin, Melville Shavelson, Jack Rose. Musical Direction by Joseph J. Lilley. Photographed by Charles B. Lang, Jr. Edited by Ellsworth Hoagland. Running time, 80 minutes.

SYNOPSIS

Freddie Hunter (*Bob Hope*) is a reporter who has been sent to Europe as counselor of a group of boy rangers. On the ocean liner he becomes involved with a card sharp (*Roland Young*), a beautiful duchess (*Rhonda Fleming*), and her impoverished father, Grand Duke Maximilian (*Roland Culver*). Detective Higgins (*Jim Backus*) is killed by the card sharp to cover up his dealings. Freddie is implicated as an accomplice and must clear himself with his youthful charges.

Roland Culver, Roland Young, and Hope

FANCY PANTS

Paramount. Released July 19, 1950.

CAST

Bob Hope, Lucille Ball, Bruce Cabot, Jack Kirkwood, Lea Penman, Hugh French, Eric Blore, Joseph Vitale, John Anderson, Norma Varden, Virginia Kelley, Colin Keith-Johnston, Joe Wong.

CREDITS

Produced by Robert Welch. Directed by George Marshall. From a novel by Harry Leon Wilson. Screenplay by Edmund Hartmann, Robert O'Brien. Musical Score by Van Cleave. Photographed by Charles B. Lang, Jr. Edited by Archie Marshek. Running time, 92 minutes.

SYNOPSIS

Agatha Floud (*Lucille Ball*), newly rich from a New Mexico cow town, has been traveling in Europe to absorb culture. She returns home with an English actor-turned-butler, Humphry (*Bob Hope*), whom the frontier townsmen take for an earl. Her father (*Jack Kirkwood*) and sweetheart (*Bruce Cabot*) try to get rid of Humphry through various means. Based loosely on *Ruggles of Red Gap*, which starred Charles Laughton in 1935.

Lucille Ball and Hope

THE LEMON DROP KID

Paramount.   Released March 8, 1951.

CAST

Bob Hope, Marilyn Maxwell, Lloyd Nolan, Jane Darwell, Andrea King, Fred Clark, Jay C. Flippen, William Frawley, Harry Bellaver, Sid Melton, Ben Weldon, Ida Moore, Francis Pierlot, Charles Cooley.

CREDITS

Produced by Robert L. Welch. Directed by Sidney Lanfield. From the story by Damon Runyon. Adaptation by Edmund Beloin. Screenplay by Edmund Hartmann, Robert O'Brien. Photographed by Daniel L. Fapp. Running time, 91 minutes.

SYNOPSIS

The Lemon Drop Kid (*Bob Hope*) is a racetrack tout who gets in trouble with bad tips at a Florida track. Moose Moran (*Fred Clark*) gives him until Christmas to make up a $10,000 error. Unable to raise the money in New York, the Kid opens an old folks' home as a ruse to license bogus Santa Clauses on the city streets. Charley (*Lloyd Nolan*) muscles in on the racket. The Kid manages to escape the heat and land both Moose and Charley in jail. The Livingston-Evans songs include "It Doesn't Cost a Dime to Dream" and "Silver Bells."

Paramount. Released Dec. 27, 1951.

CAST

Bob Hope, Hedy Lamarr, Francis L. Sullivan, Arnold Moss, Tonio Selwart, Stephen Chase, John Archer, Morris Ankrum, Marc Lawrence, Iris Adrian, Mike Mazurki, Luis Van Rooten, Ralph Smiley.

CREDITS

Produced by Paul Jones. Directed by Norman Z. McLeod. Story by Edmund Beloin, Lou Breslow. Screenplay by Edmund Hartmann, Jack Sher. Additional Dialogue by Hal Kanter. Musical Score by Victor Young. Photographed by Victor Milner. Edited by Frank Bracht. Running time, 93 minutes.

SYNOPSIS

Government agents spot a second-rate burlesque comic named Peanuts (*Bob Hope*), who bears a remarkable resemblance to a notorious spy. When the spy is wounded, Peanuts is persuaded to impersonate him on a mission to Tangier. He encounters a counterspy, Lili Danielle (*Hedy Lamarr*), and wins her over to his side. But he has less fortune with superspy Brubaker (*Francis L. Sullivan*) and his murderous cohorts. Peanuts finally beats them at their own game.

224

Hope, Marc Lawrence, Francis L. Sullivan, Mike Mazurki

MY FAVORITE SPY

SON OF PALEFACE

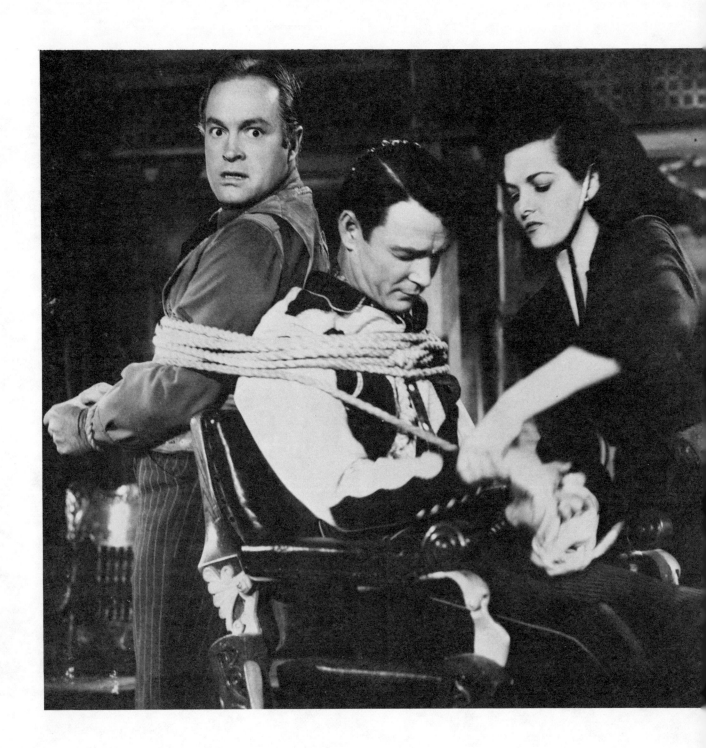

Hope, Roy Rogers, and Jane Russell

Paramount.   Released July 14, 1952.

CAST

Bob Hope, Jane Russell, Roy Rogers, Bill Williams, Lloyd Corrigan, Paul E. Burns, Douglas Dumbrille, Harry Von Zell, Iron Eyes Cody, Wee Willie Davis, Charley Cooley.

CREDITS

Produced by Robert Welch. Directed by Frank Tashlin. Screenplay by Frank Tashlin, Robert L. Welch, Joseph Quillan. Photographed by Harry J. Wild. Special Photography by Gordon Jennings, Paul Lerpae. Process Photography by Farciot Edouart. Edited by Eda Warren. Musical Score by Lyn Murray. Dance Direction by Josephine Earl. Running time, 95 minutes.

SYNOPSIS

The son of the late pioneer dentist, Painless Potter, is a callow Harvard graduate called Junior (*Bob Hope*). He goes West to claim his inheritance and becomes involved in the efforts of Roy Rogers (*Roy Rogers*) to track down a bandit who has been looting gold shipments. Suspicions center on Mike (*Jane Russell*), who runs the Dirty Shame saloon. The suspicions are correct. After a lengthy chase, Junior gets the girl and Roy Rogers remains with Trigger. Songs: "Four-legged Friend," "What a Dirty Shame," "Wing-ding Tonight," and a reprise of "Buttons and Bows."

ROAD TO BALI

Paramount.   Released Nov. 19, 1952.

CAST

   Bob Hope, Bing Crosby, Dorothy Lamour, Murvyn Vye, Peter Coe, Ralph Moody, Leon Askin.

CREDITS

   Produced by Harry Tugend. Directed by Hal Walker. Story by Frank Butler, Harry Tugend. Screenplay by Frank Butler, Hal Kanter, William Morrow. Musical Director by Joseph J. Lilley. Musical Numbers Staged by Charles O'Curran. Photography by George Barnes. Edited by Archie Marshek. Running time, 90 minutes.

SYNOPSIS

   Harold Gridley (*Bob Hope*) and George Cochran (*Bing Crosby*) are playing vaudeville in Australia but are forced to emigrate swiftly because of a pair of matrimony-minded girls. Their voyage takes them to a South Sea island where they meet Princess Lalah (*Dorothy Lamour*). She is seeking sunken treasure which rightfully belongs to her but is also being sought by the villainous Ken Arok (*Murvyn Vye*). Gridley and Cochran encounter cannibals, wild animals, and a giant squid, as well as Humphrey Bogart and Katharine Hepburn pulling *The African Queen*. Songs include "Chicago Style," "Hoot Mon," and "The Merry-Go-Runaround."

Bing Crosby, Hope, and Dorothy Lamour

Hope and Mickey Rooney (IN CAR)

OFF LIMITS

Paramount.   Released Feb. 19, 1953.

CAST

Bob Hope, Mickey Rooney, Marilyn Maxwell, Eddie Mayehoff, Stanley Clements, Jack Dempsey, Marvin Miller, John Ridgely, Tom Harmon, Norman Leavitt, Art Aragon, Kim Spalding, Jerry Hausner, Mike Mahoney.

CREDITS

Produced by Harry Tugend. Directed by George Marshall. Story by Hal Kanter. Screenplay by Hal Kanter, Jack Sher. Photographed by J. Peverell Marley. Edited by Arthur Schmidt. Running time, 89 minutes.

SYNOPSIS

Wally Hogan (*Bob Hope*) is the manager of prize fighter Bullets Bradley (*Stanley Clements*), who gets drafted into the Army. Wally's partners persuade him to enlist to look after his boy, then the partners cut him out of Bradley's fight profits. Wally develops a new fighter, Herbert Tuttle (*Mickey Rooney*), to win the championship. Wally's enthusiasm is upset by his affection for Tuttle's aunt (*Marilyn Maxwell*), who hates fighting. Tuttle wins the title by some offbeat tactics. Songs: "Military Policeman" and "All About Love."

HERE COME THE GIRLS

Paramount.   Released Oct. 22, 1953.

CAST

Bob Hope, Arlene Dahl, Rosemary Clooney, Tony Martin, Millard Mitchell, William Demarest, Fred Clark, Robert Strauss, Zamah Cunningham, Frank Orth, The Four Step Brothers, Hugh Sanders, Inesita.

CREDITS

Produced by Paul Jones. Directed by Claude Binyon. Story by Edmund Hartmann. Screenplay by Edmund Hartmann and Hal Kanter. Photographed by Lionel Lindon. Edited by Arthur Schmidt. Running time, 78 minutes.

SYNOPSIS

Stanley Snodgrass (*Bob Hope*) is an awkward chorus boy with a knack for breaking up production numbers. Fired by an irate producer (*Fred Clark*), he seems destined to seek regular employment. But he is suddenly catapulted into the lead in a musical. The reason: Jack the Slasher (*Robert Strauss*) wants to murder the real star (*Tony Martin*) because of his romance with Irene Bailey (*Arlene Dahl*). Stanley forsakes his own girl (*Rosemary Clooney*) to pursue Irene and thus become a clay pigeon. Songs include: "Ya Got Class," "Girls," "Ali Baba," "See the Circus," "It's Torment."

Arlene Dahl and Hope

CASANOVA'S BIG NIGHT

Paramount.   Released March 1, 1954

CAST

Bob Hope, Joan Fontaine, Audrey Dalton, Basil Rathbone, Hugh Marlowe, Arnold Moss, John Carradine, John Hoyt, Hope Emerson, Robert Hutton, Lon Chaney, Raymond Burr, Frieda Inescort, Primo Carnera.

CREDITS

Produced by Paul Jones. Directed by Norman Z. McLeod. Story by Aubrey Wisberg. Screenplay by Hal Kanter, Edmund Hartmann. Photographed by Lionel Lindon. Edited by Ellsworth Hoagland. Running time, 86 minutes.

SYNOPSIS

Pippo (*Bob Hope*) is a tailor's assistant who poses as Casanova. The Duchess of Castelbello (*Hope Emerson*) hires him to test the love of Elena (*Audrey Dalton*), who is engaged to the Duchess's son (*Robert Hutton*). Pippo is aided in his quest by Casanova's valet (*Basil Rathbone*) and grocer (*Joan Fontaine*), who hopes to collect on Casanova's grocery bills. All three become ensnared in the intrigue of the Doge (*Arnold Moss*).

Hope and Joan Fontaine

THE SEVEN LITTLE FOYS

Paramount.   Released May 31, 1955.

CAST

   Bob Hope, Milly Vitale, Angela Clarke, George Tobias, Billy Gray, Lee Erickson, Paul De Rolf, Linda Bennett, Lydia Reed, Tommy Duran, Jimmy Baird, James Cagney.

CREDITS

   Produced by Jack Rose. Directed by Melville Shavelson. Screenplay by Melville Shavelson, Jack Rose. Musical Direction by Joseph J. Lilley. Photographed by John F. Warren. Edited by Ellsworth Hoagland. Running time, 95 minutes.

SYNOPSIS

   Vaudevillian Eddie Foy (*Bob Hope*) swears he will always remain single, but he falls for a ballet beauty, Madeleine Morando (*Milly Vitale*). They have seven children, but he is not much of a husband and father, pursuing his career most of the time. When his wife dies, Eddie is forced to take over the family. He trains the kids to join his vaudeville act. Among the nostalgic numbers: "Mary's a Grand Old Name," "The Greatest Father of Them All," "Smiles," "Row Row, Row," "Chinatown," "Nobody," "Yankee Doodle Boy."

Milly Vitale and Hope

THAT CERTAIN FEELING

Paramount.   Released June 4, 1956.

CAST

Bob Hope, Eva Marie Saint, George Sanders, Pearl Bailey, David Lewis, Al Capp, Jerry Mathers, Herbert Rudley, Florenz Ames.

CREDITS

Produced by Norman Panama, Melvin Frank. Directed by Norman Panama, Melvin Frank. From a play by Jean Kerr, Eleanor Brooke. Screenplay by Norman Panama, Melvin Frank, I. A. L. Diamond, William Altman. Music Scored and Conducted by Joseph J. Lilley. Photographed by Loyal Griggs. Edited by Tom McAdoo. Running time, 103 minutes.

SYNOPSIS

Francis X. Dignan (*Bob Hope*) is a cartoonist whose life is blighted because he gets sick to his stomach every time he grows angry. This has destroyed his marriage to Dunreath (*Eva Marie Saint*) and made him seem like a coward. Dunreath has been working as secretary to Larry Larkin (*George Sanders*), a successful comic strip artist. He hires Francis as assistant, and Francis tries to head off his former wife's marriage to the rival. Songs: "That Certain Feeling," "Hit the Road to Dreamland," "Zing! Went the Strings of My Heart."

THE IRON PETTICOAT

Metro-Goldwyn-Mayer. Released Dec. 21 1956. (Produced in England.)

CAST

Bob Hope, Katharine Hepburn, James Robertson Justice, Robert Helpmann, David Kossoff, Alan Gifford, Paul Carpenter, Noelle Middleton, Nicholas Phipps, Sidney James, Alexander Gauge, Doris Goddard, Tutte Lemkow, Sandra Dorne, Richard Watts.

CREDITS

Produced by Betty Box. Directed by Ralph Thomas. Art Direction by Carmen Dillon. Music Composed and Directed by Benjamin Frankel. Photographed by Ernest Steward. Edited by Frederick Wilson. Running time, 87 minutes.

SYNOPSIS

A lady Russian pilot (*Katharine Hepburn*) lands her plane in the American zone of Germany and is handed over to Major Chuck Lockwood (*Bob Hope*) for conversion to democracy. He falls for her and becomes involved in Russian attempts to liquidate them both. The chase takes them to London and Moscow.

BEAU JAMES

Paramount.   Released June 7, 1957.

CAST

Bob Hope, Vera Miles, Paul Douglas, Alexis Smith, Darren McGavin, Joe Mantell, Horace MacMahon, Richard Shannon, Willis Bouchey, Sid Melton, George Jessel, Walter Catlett.

CREDITS

Produced by Jack Rose. Directed by Melville Shavelson. From the book by Gene Fowler. Screenplay by Jack Rose, Melville Shavelson. Narration by Walter Winchell. Music Arranged and Conducted by Joseph J. Lilley. Photographed by John F. Warren. Special Photographic Effects by John P. Fulton. Process Photography by Farciot Edouart. Edited by Floyd Knudtson. Running time, 105 minutes.

SYNOPSIS

Governor Al Smith (*Walter Catlett*) persuades Jimmy Walker (*Bob Hope*) to run for mayor of New York City. Walker wins, but he finds his political career in jeopardy because of his love for an actress, Betty Compton (*Vera Miles*). Walker is a Catholic and already has a wife (*Alexis Smith*). Walker tries to run the city fairly, but he falls into a financial arrangement that discredits and defeats him. Songs include such standards as "Manhattan," "Sidewalks of New York," and "Will You Love Me in December As You Do in May?"

Hope and Alexis Smith

PARIS HOLIDAY

United Artists.   Released March 7, 1958. (Produced in France.)

CAST

Bob Hope, Fernandel, Anita Ekberg, Martha Hyer, Preston Sturges, Andre Morell, Alan Gifford, Maurice Teynac, Ives Brainville, Jean Murat.

CREDITS

Produced by Robert Hope. Associate Producer, Cecil Foster Kemp. Directed by Gerd Oswald. Story by Robert Hope. Screenplay by Edmund Beloin, Dean Riesner. Music Composed and Conducted by Joseph J. Lilley. Photographed by Roger Hubert. Edited by Ellsworth Hoagland. Running time, 100 minutes.

SYNOPSIS

Robert Leslie Hunter (*Bob Hope*), an American entertainer, goes to France to acquire a French play for his next vehicle. He meets up with Fernydel (*Fernandel*), a Frenchman who plays Cupid for Hunter and Ann McCall (*Martha Hyer*), who is headed for the American Embassy. All become involved with Zara (*Anita Ekberg*), a beauteous spy. Hunter learns that the comedy he plans to acquire is in reality an exposé of a French counterfeiting ring, and he and the others become enmeshed in a lengthy chase with the culprits.

United Artists.   Released March 20, 1959.

CAST

Bob Hope, Rhonda Fleming, Wendell Corey, Jim Davis, Gloria Talbott, Will Wright, Mary Young.

CREDITS

Executive Producer, Bob Hope. Produced by Jack Hope. Directed by Norman Z. McLeod. Story by Robert St. Aubrey, Bert Lawrence. Screenplay by William Bowers, Daniel D. Beauchamp. Music Arranged and Conducted by Joseph J. Lilley. Photographed by Lionel Lindon. Special Photographic Effects by John P. Fulton. Edited by Marvin Coil, Jack Bachom. Running time, 92 minutes.

SYNOPSIS

Milford Farnsworth (*Bob Hope*) is a Coney Island insurance salesman sent West to cancel an insurance policy on the life of Jesse James (*Wendell Corey*), who is considered a poor risk. James's girl friend Cora Lee Collins (*Rhonda Fleming*) is beneficiary of the policy, and Farnsworth falls for her. James gets the idea to have the insurance man pose as himself, then be killed as Jesse James. Farnsworth discovers the plot and ends up capturing the James gang.

ALIAS JESSE JAMES

Wendell Corey, Hope, and Rhonda Fleming

THE FACTS OF LIFE

United Artists.   Released Nov. 14, 1960.

CAST

Bob Hope, Lucille Ball, Ruth Hussey, Don DeFore, Louis Nye, Philip Ober, Marianne Stewart, Peter Leeds, Hollis Irving, William Lanteau, Robert F. Simon, Louise Beavers, Mike Mazurki.

CREDITS

Produced by Norman Panama. Associate Producer, Hal C. Kern. Directed by Melvin Frank. Screenplay by Norman Panama, Melvin Frank. Music Composed and Conducted by Leigh Harline. Photographed by Charles Lang. Edited by Frank Bracht. Running time, 103 minutes.

SYNOPSIS

Larry Gilbert (*Bob Hope*) is married to Mary (*Ruth Hussey*). Kitty Weaver (*Lucille Ball*) is married to Jack (*Don DeFore*). They meet socially at the country club and seem happily married. But both Larry and Kitty are discontent with their lives and they seek escape in each other's arms. They go off for a tryst, but nothing works out as expected.

Metro-Goldwyn-Mayer.   Released Nov. 16, 1961.

CAST

Bob Hope, Lana Turner, Janis Paige, Jim Hutton, Paula Prentiss, Don Porter, Virginia Grey, Agnes Moorehead, Florence Sundstrom, Clinton Sundberg, John McGiver, Alan Hewitt, Reta Shaw.

CREDITS

Produced by Ted Richmond. Directed by Jack Arnold. Story by Vera Caspary. Screenplay by Valentine Davies, Hal Kanter. Musical Score by Henry Mancini. Photographed by Joseph Ruttenberg. Edited by Richard W. Farrell. Running time, 109 minutes.

SYNOPSIS

Adam J. Niles (*Bob Hope*) is a best-selling author who runs into trouble with the government when an aide disappears without paying Niles's income tax. His publisher advises him to write a book on how America lives, so the author moves into Paradise Hill Village, disguises himself, and begins researching among the housewives. He falls for Rosemary Howard (*Lana Turner*), who works in the development office. Local husbands led by Thomas Jynson (*Don Porter*) become suspicious of Niles and try to run him out of the neighborhood.

BACHELOR IN PARADISE

ROAD TO HONG KONG

United Artists. Released May 22, 1962. (Produced in England.)

CAST

Bing Crosby, Bob Hope, Joan Collins, Dorothy Lamour, Robert Morley, Walter Gotell, Roger Delgado, Felix Aylmer, Peter Madden, Alan Gifford, Robert Ayres, Robin Hughes, Julian Sherrier, Bill Nagy, Guy Standeven, John McCarthy, Simon Levy, Jacqueline Jones, Victor Brooks, Roy Patrick, John Dearth, David Randall, Michael Wynne, Mei Ling, Katya Douglas, Harry Baird, Irving Allen, Yvonne Shima, Camilla Brockman, Lena Margot, Sheree Winton, Edwina Carroll, Diane Valentine, April Ashley, Jacqueline Leigh, Sein Short, Lier Hwang, Michelle Molk, Zoe Zephyr.

CREDITS

Produced by Melvin Frank. Directed by Norman Panama. Screenplay by Norman Panama, Melvin Frank. Music Composed and Conducted by Robert Farnon. Songs by Sammy Cahn, Jimmy Van Heusen. Photographed by Jack Hilyard. Supervising Film Editor, Alan Osbiston. Edited by John Smith. Running time, 91 minutes.

SYNOPSIS

Chester Babcock (*Bob Hope*) and Harry Turner (*Bing Crosby*) are on the run in Hong Kong and blunder into a vaudeville act which stars Dorothy Lamour (*Dorothy Lamour*). Babcock loses his memory and the two adventurers become involved with a pretty spy, Diane (*Joan Collins*), plus a wacky group of thugs called the Third Echelon, led by the Leader (*Robert Morley*). The chase includes everything from rickshaws to space capsules. Frank Sinatra, Dean Martin, David Niven, Zsa Zsa Gabor, Peter Sellers, and Jerry Colonna make brief appearances. Songs include "Teamwork."

Hope, Joan Collins, and Bing Crosby

CRITIC'S CHOICE

Hope, Jessie Royce Landis and Lucille Ball

Warner Bros.   Released April 13, 1963.

CAST

Bob Hope, Lucille Ball, Marilyn Maxwell, Rip Torn, Jessie Royce Landis, John Dehner, Jim Backus, Ricky Kelman, Dorothy Green, Marie Windsor, Evan McCord, Richard Deacon, Joan Shawlee, Donald Losby, Lurene Tuttle, Ernestine Wade, Stanley Adams, Jerome Cowan.

CREDITS

Produced by Frank P. Rosenberg. Directed by Don Weis. From the play by Ira Levin. Screenplay by Jack Sher. Musical Score by George Duning. Orchestration by Arthur Morton. Photographed by Charles Lang. Edited by William Ziegler. Running time, 100 minutes.

SYNOPSIS

Broadway critic Parker Ballentine (*Bob Hope*) is faced with the crisis of reviewing a play written by his wife Angela (*Lucille Ball*). He solves it by showing up at the premiere drunk and creating a disturbance. Then he writes a devastating review, which causes havoc in his marriage.

United Artists.   Released June 14, 1963. (Produced in England.)

CAST

Bob Hope, Anita Ekberg, Edie Adams, Lionel Jeffries, Arnold Palmer, Percy Herbert, Paul Carpenter, Bari Jonson, Orlando Martins, Al Mulock, Peter Dyneley, Mai Ling, Mark Heath.

CREDITS

Executive Producer, Harry Staltzman. Produced by Albert R. Broccoli. Associate Producer, Stanley Sopel. Directed by Gordon Douglas. Screenplay by Nate Monaster, Johanna Harwood. Musical Score by Muir Mathieson, Monty Norman. Music Conducted by Muir Mathieson. Title song by Monty Norman. Photographed by Ted Moore. Edited by Peter Hunt. Running time, 103 minutes.

SYNOPSIS

Matt Merriwether (*Bob Hope*) is a bogus explorer who has written books of African adventures based on the exploits of his uncle. An American moon-probe capsule lands in Africa, and the government enlists Merriwether to find it before enemy nations. He reluctantly goes to Africa, accompanied by a secret agent, Frederica Larsen (*Edie Adams*). They encounter an enemy spy, Luba (*Anita Ekberg*), and fellow agent Ezra Mungo (*Lionel Jeffries*), who poses as a missionary.

CALL ME BWANA

Lionel Jeffries, Anita Ekberg, Hope, and Edie Adams

A GLOBAL AFFAIR

Metro-Goldwyn-Mayer.   Released Jan. 30, 1964.

CAST

Bob Hope, Lilo Pulver, Michele Mercier, Elga Andersen, Yvonne De Carlo, Miiko Taka, Robert Sterling, Nehemiah Persoff, John McGiver, Jacques Bergerac, Mickey Shaughnessy.

CREDITS

Produced by Hall Bartlett. Associate Producer, Eugene Vale. Directed by Jack Arnold. Story by Eugene Vale. Screenplay by Arthur Marx, Bob Fisher, Charles Lederer. Musical Score by Dominic Frontiere. Photographed by Joseph L. Ruttenberg. Edited by Bud Molin. Running time, 84 minutes.

SYNOPSIS

Frank Larrimore (*Bob Hope*) is a United Nations department head who discovers a baby in the UN building. Since that is international territory, the abandoned waif becomes the center of politically motivated competition for various countries to adopt the child. Ladies of various nationalities seek to persuade Larrimore to favor their countries, but he decides to adopt the baby himself as "the world's first truly international citizen."

Hope and baby

United Artists. Released June 2, 1965.

CAST

Bob Hope, Tuesday Weld, Frankie Avalon, Dina Merrill, Jeremy Slate, Rosemarie Frankland, Walter Sande, John Qualen, Peter Bourne, Fay De Witt, Alice Frost, Roy Roberts.

CREDITS

Produced by Edward Small. Associate Producer, Alex Gottlieb. Directed by Frederick De Cordova. Story by Nat Perrin. Screenplay by Nat Perrin, Bob Fisher, Arthur Marx. Music by Jimmie Haskell, By Dunham. Music Conducted by Jimmie Haskell. Photographed by Daniel L. Fapp. Supervising Film Editor, Grant Whytock. Running time, 96 minutes.

SYNOPSIS

Bob Holcomb (*Bob Hope*) is a widower with a daughter JoJo (*Tuesday Weld*). He doesn't approve of her friends, especially beau Kenny Klinger (*Frankie Avalon*), who rides a motorcycle. Holcomb arranges to be transferred to Sweden. There JoJo falls for a suave playboy (*Jeremy Slate*), and Holcomb becomes involved with an interior decorator (*Dina Merrill*). The alarmed father brings Klinger from California to attempt breaking up the liaison with the playboy. Songs include "I'll Take Sweden," "Watusi Joe," "The Bells Keep Ringing," "Take It Off," "There'll Be Rainbows Again."

Tuesday Weld, Frankie Avalon, Hope, and Dina Merrill

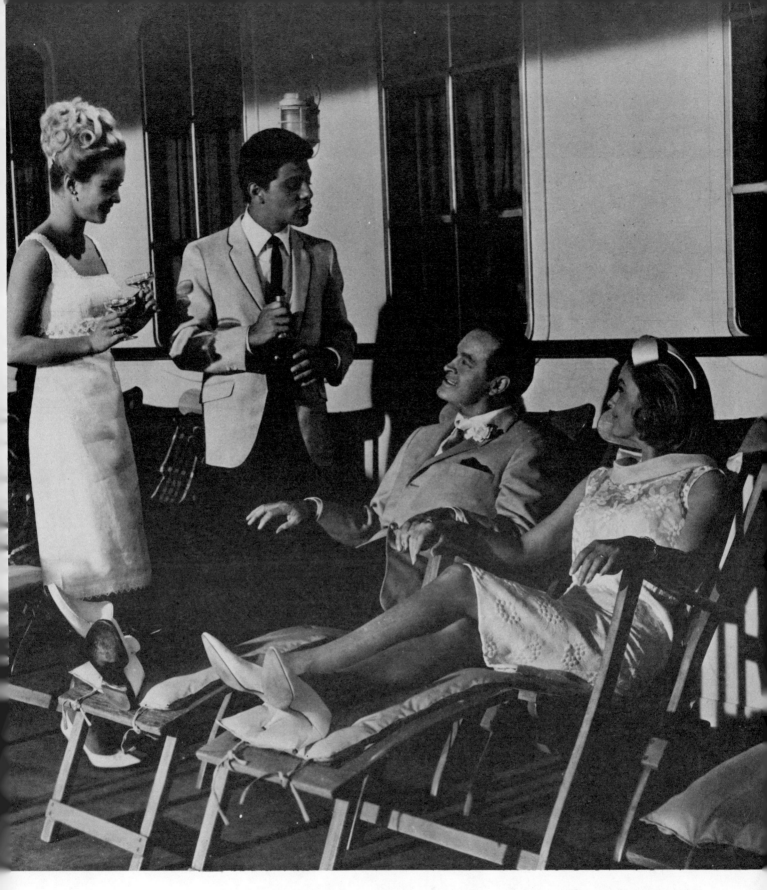

I'LL TAKE SWEDEN

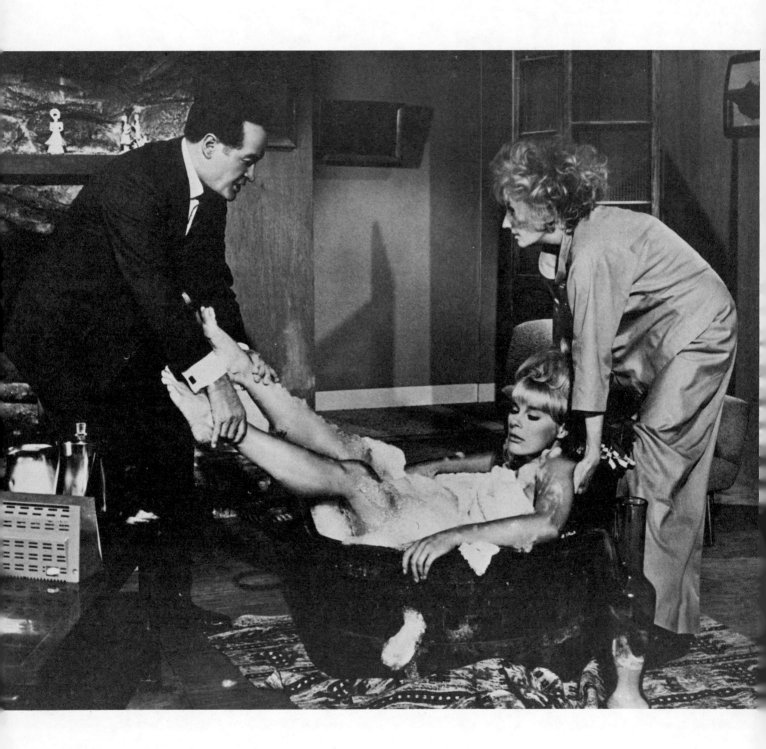

Hope, Elke Sommer, and Phyllis Diller

BOY, DID I GET A WRONG NUMBER!

United Artists.   Released June 1, 1966.

CAST

Bob Hope, Elke Sommer, Phyllis Diller, Cesare Danova, Marjorie Lord, Kelly Thorsden, Benny Baker, Terry Burnham, Joyce Jameson, Harry Von Zell, Kevin Burchett, Keith Taylor, John Todd Roberts.

CREDITS

Produced by Edward Small. Directed by George Marshall. Story by George Beck. Screenplay by Burt Styler, Albert E. Lewin, George Kennett. Photographed by Lionel Lindon. Music by Richard LaSalle, By Dunham. Edited by Grant Whytock. Running time, 99 minutes.

SYNOPSIS

Real estate man Tom Meade (*Bob Hope*) dials a wrong number and becomes connected with a glamorous film star, Didi (*Elke Sommer*). She has taken refuge in his Oregon town to escape her boy friend, film director Pepe (*Cesare Danova*). When her car is found in a lake, Meade is accused of her murder, and his problems are compounded by his wacky maid (*Phyllis Diller*).

United Artists.   Released April 4, 1967.

CAST

Bob Hope, Phyllis Diller, Jonathan Winters, Shirley Eaton, Jill St. John, Stacey Maxwell, Kevin Brody, Robert Hope, Glenn Gilger, Avis Hope, Debi Storm, Michael Freeman, Austin Willis, Peter Leeds.

CREDITS

Associate Producer, Bill Lawrence. Directed by George Marshall. Story by Bob Fisher, Arthur Marx. Screenplay by Albert E. Lewin, Burt Styler, Bob Fisher, Arthur Marx. Photographed by Alan Stensvold. Music by George Romanis. Edited by Frank Baur. Running time, 106 minutes.

SYNOPSIS

Widower Henry Dimsdale (*Bob Hope*) is a bank teller with seven children and an unpaid housekeeper Golda (*Phyllis Diller*). Finding $10,000 in a parking lot, he buys a new car. A $50,000 embezzlement is discovered in his books at the bank, and Dimsdale is persuaded by friends to flee until he can find a way to clear himself. He takes off with the seven kids and their Newfoundland dog, pursued by the police and Detective Jasper Lynch (*Jonathan Winters*), boy friend of Golda.

EIGHT ON THE LAM

Jill St. John and Hope

266

THE PRIVATE NAVY OF SGT. O'FARRELL

United Artists.   Released May 8, 1968.

CAST

Bob Hope, Phyllis Diller, Jeffrey Hunter, Gina Lollobrigida, Mylene Demongeot, John Myhers, Mako, Henry Wilcoxon, Dick Sargent, Christopher Dark, Michael Burns, William Wellman, Jr., Robert Donner, Jack Grinnage, William Christopher, John Spina.

CREDITS

Produced by John Beck. Directed by Frank Tashlin. Story by John L. Greene, Robert M. Fresco. Screenplay by Frank Tashlin. Photographed by Alan Stensvold. Music by Harry Stikman. Edited by Eda Warren. Running time, 92 minutes.

SYNOPSIS

The scene is a South Pacific island which has been bypassed by the war. Sgt. O'Farrell (*Bob Hope*) is seeking a cargo ship loaded with beer which has been torpedoed. He is concerned over the troops' morale. During his mission he encounters a wacky nurse (*Phyllis Diller*), a Japanese soldier (*Mako*), and a former sweetheart (*Gina Lollobrigida*) who has been shipwrecked. He also manages to capture a Japanese submarine.

Hope and shipmates

HOW TO COMMIT MARRIAGE

Tim Matthieson, Hope, and Jackie Gleason

Cinerama.   Released May 28, 1971.

CAST

Bob Hope, Jackie Gleason, Jane Wyman, Maureen Arthur, Leslie Nielsen, Tina Louise, Paul Stewart, Irwin Corey, Joanna Cameron, Tim Matthieson, The Comfortable Chair.

CREDITS

Produced by Bill Lawrence. Directed by Norman Panama. Screenplay by Ben Starr, Michael Kanin. Photographed by Charles Lang. Music by Joseph J. Lilley. Rock numbers by The Comfortable Chair. Edited by Ronald Sinclair. Running time, 98 minutes.

SYNOPSIS

Frank and Elaine Benson (*Bob Hope, Jane Wyman*) have decided on a divorce. But then their daughter Nancy (*Joanna Cameron*) comes home from college to announce that she is marrying David Poe (*Tim Matthieson*). He is the son of a cynical rock-show promoter, Oliver Poe (*Jackie Gleason*). When Nancy finds out about her parents' split, she decides to skip marriage and move in with David. The pair join a rock group, she becomes pregnant and puts the baby up for adoption. The grandparents adopt the child, complicating their own romances with other partners.

270   Eva Marie Saint, Betty Ann Carr, and Hope

CANCEL MY RESERVATION

Warner Bros.   Released Oct. 15, 1972.

CAST

   Bob Hope, Eva Marie Saint, Ralph Bellamy, Forrest Tucker, Keenan Wynn, Doodles Weaver, Betty Ann Carr, Henry Darrow, Chief Dan George, Anne Archer, Herb Vigran, Pat Morita, Roy Rowan, Suzanne Beaumont, Gordon Oliver, Paul Bogart, Buster Shaver, Marsha Umberhaur.

CREDITS

   Executive Producer, Bob Hope. Assistant, Bill Lawrence. Produced by Gordon Oliver. Directed by Paul Bogart. Screenplay by Arthur Marx and Robert Fisher. Photographed by Russell L. Metty. Music by Dominic Frontiere. Edited by Michael Hoey. Running time, 95 minutes.

SYNOPSIS

   Dan and Sheila Bartlett (*Bob Hope* and *Eva Marie Saint*) conduct a daytime television show in New York. They come into conflict over women's rights, and a doctor advises Dan to seek a rest, alone. He goes off to his ranch in Arizona and becomes implicated when the body of a dead Indian girl is found in his car. In trying to exonerate himself, Dan becomes more deeply involved in an intrigue involving a wealthy landowner (*Ralph Bellamy*) and the Indians.

Hope has also made guest appearances in such features as *The Greatest Show on Earth*, Paramount, 1952; *Scared Stiff*, Paramount, 1953; *The Five Pennies*, Paramount, 1959; and *The Oscar*, Embassy, 1966.